OVER-THE-TOP

OVER-THE-TOP

A "P.B.I." IN THE H.A.C.

By
ARTHUR LAMBERT

SECOND IMPRESSION

London
John Long, Limited
34, 35 & 36 Paternoster Row
[*All rights reserved*]

OVER-THE-TOP
A "P.B.I." IN THE H.A.C.

By
ARTHUR LAMBERT

SECOND IMPRESSION

London
John Long, Limited
34, 35 & 36 Paternoster Row
[All rights reserved]

TO
THE "BOYS"
PAST AND PRESENT

FOREWORD

THIS is not a war novel. Every incident is as true as a battered memory, aided by a scrappy Diary, will allow. Long, and possibly wearisome, as it is, thousands of incidents have been omitted.

Every effort has been made to disguise disgust at men and systems that were insults to intelligence, and to tone down descriptions of scenes inconceivably ghastly. Little attempt has been made to reproduce the emotions that filled the mind and heart of every private soldier, to a greater or lesser degree, during those agonising years, and none whatever to foster the delusion that men went cheerfully to battle. On the other hand, every possible instance of bravery and cheerfulness has been recorded.

This narrative was commenced after the war, in the "joy room" known as the "Imst-attic," Tyrol; was continued in various billets and "gasthofs" in that chilly little town; it helped to pass the tedium of the long truck journeys to Havre, and was completed in an office near St. Paul's Cathedral. It camouflages as skilfully as possible two years of mental and physical misery, for which the enemy was not wholly blamed.

CONTENTS

BOOK ONE
FRANCE AND FLANDERS

CHAPTER		PAGE
I.	ENGLAND	17
II.	HAVRE	26
III.	QUELMES	32
IV.	ZILLEBEKE	37
V.	"AMMUNITION AND DUCK-BOARDS"	41
VI.	"JOLTING HORSE" TRENCH	49
VII.	BROODSEINDE RIDGE	54
VIII.	GETTING OUT!	62
IX.	"REWARDS" AT METEREN	68
X.	THE STRETCHER-BEARING "STUNT"	75
XI.	GHELUVELT	78
XII.	FAREWELL TO FLANDERS	87

BOOK TWO
ITALY

I.	"IN THE TRAIN"	91
II.	A WALK ACROSS ITALY	97
III.	HOME COMFORTS AT RAMON	102

CONTENTS

CHAPTER		PAGE
IV.	NERVESA	112
V.	IN HOSPITAL	117
VI.	"WIND-UP" AND DOWN	122
VII.	MULES!	128
VIII.	UP AND DOWN THE MOUNTAINS	140
IX.	ALMOST A "REST"	144
X.	CLIMBING TO THE FRONT LINE	149
XI.	THE ROYAL REVIEW	154
XII.	THE AUSTRIAN OFFENSIVE	158
XIII.	A BUSY WEEK	163
XIV.	CONCERTS IN THE MOUNTAINS	173
XV.	A REAL REST	178
XVI.	AMONG THE OUTPOSTS	182
XVII.	THE FOUR-PLATOON DINNER	189
XVIII.	"GRAVE DI PAPADOPOLI"	196
XIX.	CHASING THE CHASERS	202

BOOK THREE

AUSTRIA

I.	"BATTALION IN OCCUPATION"	211
II.	DEMOBILISATION	218

BOOK ONE
FRANCE AND FLANDERS

CHAPTER I

ENGLAND

BACK in the far-distant year of Nineteen Hundred and Seventeen, the people of England were in a daze of indecision and misery.

The Great War had long outlived the fallacy of a short and sharp campaign. Fighting was continuous on a dozen fronts and the outstanding battles of Loos, the Somme and the Ancre had produced nothing more definite than hideous lists of casualties, and ever-increasing additions to black-clad and sorrowful civilians.

The Ypres salient was a nightmare to be mentioned with bated breath, and Zeppelins had appeared over England, gleaming like silver sharks to the awed eyes of the scared observers.

The young men had departed overseas long since. Young girls were doing their work, and were assisting those millions of men making munitions, whose inarticulate sorrow was being expressed in mutterings and occasional howls of rage at the number of hours and the rate of pay.

In the offices, the men who had passed their youth were digging themselves in. Some were succeeding in being regarded as indispensables, a few were suffering the opprobrium that accompanied the convictions of conscientious objectors, but the vast majority were vaguely conscious that the time was approaching when age, business, and family ties would no longer be regarded as a bar to military service.

Arthur Lambert was typical of this class. His thirty-fourth birthday was approaching, and from the day of his departure from a church Grammar School he had never indulged in anything more strenuous than the occasional week-end golf or tennis that his busy life in Fleet Street permitted. Of late, several nights a week had been spent with the local Volunteer Corps, but except for this indefinite, and rather casual form of military service, he had never fired a gun or marched along a road in his life. The idea of killing, or being killed, was so remote from his quiet, orderly life that the mere thought left him bewildered.

For a number of years he had been trying to build up a business of his own, and, strengthened by a fine experience in large publishing firms, was slowly but surely carving a niche in the granite surface of success. Profits were not large, but were maintaining a charming wife and three healthy infants in that comfortable middle-class way to which they had become accustomed.

There had never been any acute shortage of money in the Lambert family, nor any lack of good food, clothing, or amusements, and certainly no experience of hardships, exposure, danger, or physical or mental exhaustion.

Now Lambert had to face them all. A tribunal had intimated that he must go and serve his country. His business must be left to take care of itself, his wife must protect the home and children with the help of God and the Civil Liabilities authorities, and he must exchange his known life of sedentary work for the unknown experiences of the man in khaki.

He was physically fit, and there was no question of home service, or the inflated ranks of the artillery, yeomanry or other units, where men rode instead of walked. A commission was out of the question. The ever-increasing vacancies in the officers' ranks were being filled by men with experience of active service,

ENGLAND

and the lists of the Officers' Training Corps were completely closed to men without the advantages of a Public School education or influence. There was nothing for it but the ranks of some infantry unit.

Several regiments in London were recruiting from the business classes, but even in their cases it was no easy matter to join them, and it was like a gleam of sunshine through the murk of a foggy day when Lambert was accepted by the respected and ancient Honourable Artillery Company.

An accomplished tenor singer had introduced him to an accomplished baritone singer, occupying an official position in the regiment, and he had been interviewed and questioned by a redoubtable body of distinguished-looking men who accepted him as a member. He was ordered to report to the Tower of London, and one day tramped home in heavier boots, coarser cloth and stiffer straps than he had ever imagined it possible to assume.

Arthur Lambert was now Private Lambert, No. 10726, 2nd Battn. H.A.C.

.   .   .   .   .   .

The first few nights at the Tower in iron cots and straw "biscuits" were the worst he had ever spent, the drill evolutions in the dirty grit of the Moat were problems that soon became mechanical, the physical "jerks" amusing and rendered easier by regular cricket in the past, and golf of recent years. Lining up for army stew and dumplings served on enamelled tins offended fastidious tastes, but all the unaccustomed roughness was forgotten when four o'clock arrived and he was free to rush home, or stroll leisurely to his City office, where the business struggled on gamely under the direction of one of those splendid "over agers" who saved thousands of firms.

Discipline was not irksome. The junior N.C.O.'s were chummy and helpful, the seniors more reserved but generally long-suffering and appreciative of earnest effort. Officers seemed afar off, and the tremendously tall, thin, Regimental-Sergeant-Major, with the roar of a lion, became a being of flesh and blood when he frisked boyishly with the sergeants during the welcome breaks in the training.

Route marches to Charing Cross or Hyde Park were dreadful in comparison with strolls across Hampstead Heath or toddles with the children. Lambert found the roads hot; the smell of petrol suffocating; and the stares of lady-shoppers revived the boyish self-consciousness that seemed to have lost its terrors years before. It was exhausting work, but Lambert never dreamed of the marches to come, with loads worthy of mules, over roads so dreadful that the Strand became a street of dreams !

Even at that early stage the recruits made the best of the job by singing popular songs or inquiring at pertinent moments : " Who were the men who went on strike ? Hoo ! Ha ! Hoo ! Ha ! Ha ! " or selecting any name from a facia and roaring in unison " Good mor-rning, Mister Blank," in the manner familiarised by " The Roosters."

Schooldays returned during the nights at the Tower. Shadowy forms darted into long dormitories after " lights out " and a dozer collapsed amidst the ruins of his bed, and Lambert felt a " cocky " thrill run through his veins when a struggling ghost was captured in a hefty tackle and he assisted in the resultant ducking.

The departure of squads for other training grounds was a good excuse for revels at terrible hours. Some lasted as late as ten " pip emma " when song followed song, and speech speech until the entertainment reached a finale with two corporals and three privates delivering orations together. The " spirit " of the H.A.C. was a great feature of these entertainments.

Gathered in from all the professions and arts that

exist, the supply of talent during those days was constant and delightful. Dressed in pants and shirt, sweet singers stood on beds and delighted all with ballads, fascinated with recitations, or kept a room hanging on each note from violin or guitar. France, Italy and Austria were before the " awkward squad " but no music ever came from estaminet, or vine-covered billet to equal those nights in the musty Tower.

Sore throats and frightful arms were the first tests of pain for the new soldiers. They do not take first place in the terrors of training, as " Inoculation leave " took Lambert and Co. home for a few days to sleep in a high fever, but a soft bed, eat meals wonderfully tasty and beautifully served, and to walk familiar roads with a more erect carriage and a fearfully heavy tread.

Squad drill and physical "jerks" at the Tower merely educated the recruit in obedience, and developed those muscles that had been lying dormant. There was little or no suggestion of war there, but it came with the removal to " The Cedars " at Blackheath, for the intensive, hectic second stage.

In the delightful grounds of that house, bayonet fighting, field training, advancing in artillery formation or bombing attacks in miniature trenches followed hot and fast on one another's heels. Fierce night attacks took place at six o'clock on warm spring evenings, and Lambert became acquainted with the " tin hat," which was to be such a heavy, but morally comfortable companion in the near future. He was trained in the rapid fixing of gas masks, to be prepared for the foulest method of killing your enemy that the Devil ever devised, and route-marched in full pack that seemed cutting and crushing after previous loads.

In spite of the heavy strain that the frenzied training imposed upon his older physique, and the mental strain of his present and future position, Lambert found it all rather good fun, but he was to have a foretaste of the effect of discipline upon his temperament.

A small corporal of about eighteen years disliked the way Lambert obeyed some trivial order, and repeated it in a staccato voice that sent the blood surging to the private's head. With the earth revolving, and eyes bulging, Lambert consigned the corporal, his orders and threats to the uttermost ends of the hottest Inferno, and quelled the superior with the fury of his outburst.

This period was not without other portents. During physical "jerks" one fine morning, when the parade ground was covered with squads of men in various states of undress, urgent orders were given to the men to seek immediate cover. A few seconds later a flock resembling silver gulls flew over. They were at an immense height but the sun gleamed on the metal chassis of aeroplanes flying in excellent formation towards the centre of London.

There was an interval of breathless silence, and then the reports of heavy explosions reached the men's ears as the flying murderers scuttled back with the English avengers hard on their track. Soon after an aeroplane with red, white and blue circles hurtled to earth like a shot pheasant.

It was the first daylight raid—the first foul shot in the campaign of slaughter of defenceless non-combatants that the Germans were to wage.

One day out of the crowd of "rookies" there emerged Draft 24 and a curious tingling ran down Lambert's spine when his name was called. For the first time for six weeks he realised that his time was coming, and through his brain rushed the knowledge that home, wife and children and business were soon to be left, and that he was to prove his manhood in other fields.

From that minute life changed for Draft 24. Spare

hours were spent by most of them in making every possible arrangement for preserving business assets, and enjoying the pleasures of London at the same time. Little mention of the trip " over there " was made but it was present in every man's mind, and the hurried meetings with wife, sweetheart, or mother were melancholy beneath the camouflage of hilarity.

Friendships commenced with the draft that survived the strongest test of masculine affinity God has devised —the sharing with other men of burning heat and bitter cold ; little food and less luxury ; mud and murder ; vermin and exhaustion.

Lambert took his wife to the seaside for the four days " draft leave." Eight years had passed since his honeymoon and it seemed fitting that his married life should end, if end it must, in the way it began.

Emotion is *infra dig* to the English, and these two people displayed none. They laughed, walked, bathed and basked with little reference to next week, and few realised how deep ran the undercurrent of feeling. Always calm and self-contained, Lambert's wife tripped gracefully along the promenades with the sun glinting in her golden hair and a merry smile on her lips, and only on the morning of parting was there a glimpse of her real feelings.

Lambert was detailing the financial arrangements that were the best that he had been able to make in the short time. Both knew them by heart, but something had to be said. Silence was unthinkable ! The man started some foolish sentence, scarcely aware of the words when the storm broke. Tears filled the brown eyes and heavy sobs shook the woman's frame.

Lambert led his wife to the large room where the two elder boys slept. They had been awake, discussing excitedly the splendid thing happening in their house. Now, as they saw their mother's grief, small mouths drooped, the younger jumped impulsively into his mother's arms and both commenced to cry. Lambert talked bravely of returning soon. He did not feel it. Four brothers were in the Army, none killed, and his logical mind could not conceive immunity for all of them, but cheerfulness was vital. Damn it! he must not cry.

A few hurried words and a visit to his own room where his youngest boy lay in a welter of golden curls, his face angelic in sleep. A tender kiss on the chubby lips and then down into the hall, followed by a tragic figure of woe.

Waving of hands and a wet handkerchief and a dozen turnabouts until Private Lambert disappeared from view, his eyes dry but his heart bursting. All the world was dull and black. The folk he loved and treasured left to grieve alone. All the work and thought of fifteen years lost in the whirlpool of the cursed war.

Back at Blackheath the members of Draft 24 grinned pathetically at one another that night. In low tones, newly won pals epitomised recent farewells in one word " Awful ! "

There were few relatives at Waterloo the next morning. A consensus of opinion tabooed public embraces and tears and the general public were not admitted.

Lambert obtained permission to go outside the barriers to change English money to French and received cheery remarks from worthy but outspoken persons. A hand gripped his, and pump-handled it vigorously, and he gazed into the mournful face of an elderly employee. He thanked him heartily for coming and the old man tried hard to reply, but tears choked him and there was an embarrassing interval.

" Pore old man," came from the crowd that immediately collected. " Never mind, dad. Yore son'll come back. 'E's one of our 'eroes, mind yer."

Lambert escaped precipitately and rejoined the draft. It was the time for camouflage and he dashed into wild spirits. . . . Forgotten jokes rose in his memory; he bawled out snatches of songs; chipped all and sundry and roused the emulation of the whole draft. Laughter and fun came to many a man's rescue that morning. As the train moved out, some fellow's charming sister ran to the carriage window.

"I think you are showing the true H.A.C. spirit," she said to Lambert.

"Thank you," he returned. "I wish we had some in a bottle."

It was a rude retort, but feelings were not normal, and the train steamed out, as thousands had done, with recruits cheering at the top of their voices, trying to drown the lumps that were rising very high in their throats.

CHAPTER II

HAVRE

THE sun was tipping the ripples of water in Southampton Dock as Draft 24 lay on the stones, surrounded by piles of equipment. They had been there for hours and were likely to be there for hours yet. Nobody seemed to know the programme, there were no officers or civilians or troopships in sight, and those ripples of blue water kept rolling in, tipped with silver and gold. The men were abstracted and busy with their inward thoughts.

It was Lambert who suggested a swim in the dock, and in a second dozens of men had stripped and were splashing about in the blue water like a school of porpoises. Their shouts of delighted laughter rent the weird silence of those great docks and for an hour the new soldiers, mother naked, forgot the future under the soothing influence of English sea water. There was not a towel amongst them, but the ration shirts were made of good thick flannel, and as they finished dressing a large, dirty troopship rounded the end of the dock.

As the dusk of a long day deepened *The Midland Drover* ambled into darkness and heavy rain, which continued through a long night. She had evidently been a cattle-boat, or had been adapted for carrying animals since the war started. Horse boxes ran along each side of the deck, the lower deck was full of them and the sense of smell made uncertainty impossible.

The only accommodation for men was in the spacious

hold, and into this crowded a thousand men with their tons of equipment, rifles and packs. Hardy Northerners, cheek by jowl with weedy Londoners, stocky Welshmen and tall Scots. All had donned damp and filthy lifebelts and now prepared to sleep in any and every available spot. They lay in lines, heaps and lumps, and Lambert, peering through the fog that rose slowly from the mass of bodies, marvelled how quickly most of them slept. Only once or twice in the ensuing months could he sleep quickly or continuously.

In an hour the atmosphere of that hold was thick and stinking. Lambert felt his head reeling and charged precipitately for the stairway, unheeding the muffled curses from men upon whom he trod. It was pitch dark on deck; the only lights the twinkling signals from the escorting destroyers, and he fell heavily on the wet boards, rubbing himself sympathetically in the civilian habit that was soon to fall away like many another.

A remark in a familiar accent attracted him, and he found himself in one of the horse stalls. It stank of urine, but anything was better than the hold, and he lay down on the ridged floor which pressed into his body in the places left vacant by the lifebelt, and dozed intermittently, his mind full of sick longing for England, until the grey dawn revealed the docks and wharves of Havre.

Hours later, the long column of fours clattered over the cobbles of the great French port. It wound slowly through the suburbs leading to historic Harfleur, where the great base camp was pitched in the valley of the Lazaire.

Packs were dreadfully heavy. At the suggestion of draft sergeants, the contents had been cut down to a minimum and cleaning materials had been ruthlessly "dumped." "No button cleaning at the front" had been the tale, and never did men receive more misleading advice. The residue was still appallingly heavy and every man breathed easier at the sight of white tents.

There were thousands of them pitched on the steep side of a large hill and stretching line upon line for over a mile. On one side a precipitous wooded slope, on the other fields and brooks with villas dotted here and there. A strong smell met them and the hum of a great crowd. Both grew as they marched to the middle of the camp until the odour became almost overpowering to Lambert's sensitive stomach, and the noise reminded him of Hampstead Heath on August Bank Holiday.

He never rose so early in his life as in the next week or two. Five o'clock every morning saw the various units paraded for roll call, followed by uncomfortable ablutions in packed sheds. Breakfast followed, and the feeding of ten thousand men was a revelation to the recruits. Units filed into the great dining-halls in pre-arranged order, and first turn for the H.A.C. invariably produced howls from other detachments.

Despite a record of hard fighting since December, 1914, good comradeship with all and sundry, and manliness second to none in this wicked old world, nothing could alter the general opinion that the H.A.C. were "base-wallahs" and "scroungers."

Lambert soon found that good manners did not pay at meal times. The "after you, sir!" did not work. Wait for the next man and presto! all was gone. He learnt to look after himself after one or two very light meals.

After breakfast, all the troops paraded and marched off for their day's training. A large plateau on top of a steep hill overhanging the camp was an admirable ground for manœuvres, but getting there involved a steep climb to the top of the "Pimple" and few were the men who arrived with wind to spare at the top. Draft 24 made a feature of keeping in step to popular tunes, much to the openly expressed disgust of the others, but the intense surprise at the universal resentment to all their acts soon died away into careless indifference.

Thirty thousand men learnt the advanced lessons of war on the " Pimple." They bayoneted, manœuvred and trained from seven in the morning until four in the afternoon, with a midday meal of tea, cheese and biscuit. They listened to the most bloodthirsty lectures ever conceived, from the lips of hard-bitten instructors who had seen everything since Mons.

The work was exhausting, but the air was fresh and clean, and Lambert felt the blood course strongly through his veins at the combination of incessant exercise and red-hot words from fighters' lips. He did not want to die for his wife and boys' sake, but one mad rush to those enemy trenches! . . .

In their leisure, soldiers are fond of a harmless gamble called " House," in which each player receives a card with several lines of numbers, and the promotor recites the numbers from wooden discs which he draws from a bag. There is an entrance fee for each game and the players cover any numbers on their card which happen to be called. The fortunate player who first gets all his numbers covered howls " House " at the top of his voice and if audited and found correct receives the agreed prize and the game starts all over again.

This was the only gambling game sanctioned in the Army and it was in full swing at Harfleur. The singsong of hundreds of numbers rose and fell in dreary monotone and seemed to blend itself in some way with the smell of the burning excreta, until Lambert wanted to scream.

The odour and noise jangled every sensitive nerve in his body and he fled on every possible occasion. A book, or writing-pad, in a spot high above the camp; a stroll outside the lines; an occasional pass to Havre with a lovely dip in the sea, or a visit to Harfleur Cathedral. Anywhere to escape from 8 I.B.D.

He became used to the rats that ran over his face,

or sneezed in his ears, but early and full acquaintance with the lice did not abate in the slightest the irritation and horror their presence produced. Those foul, blood-sucking, disease-carrying parasites drove every soldier to distraction until he died, was gently placed in hospital sheets, or burnt every stitch of underclothing the instant he arrived home on leave. Fair clean skins were soon scratched into a bleeding collection of skin and blotches, and every day, wet or fine, hot or cold, underclothing and tunics were searched inch by inch. There seemed no remedy for foul prolific insects and Lambert only met one man who was not tortured by them.

Each Sunday morning Lambert marched with the Roman Catholic soldiers to the cathedral. On the first occasion several thousand Australians filed in first and filled every seat and corner. The R.C. service was at nine and the C.O.E. was at eleven. The Australians had turned Catholics to a man for the sake of an extra two hours in Havre.

Lambert forgave them freely. To the invariable "Colonel Bogey" march, drafts of tall, loose-limbed, bronzed Colonials loped past the H.A.C. lines several times a day on the way "up," and he saw them later at Ypres, alive and dead.

Men were leaving the Base camps at all hours of the day and night. The demand for them from a hundred regiments was incessant, and the recruits no sooner made friends than they were whisked away into the unknown. A dozen times men came to Lambert's tent, and departed for places of terrible repute before *his own call came.*

His false teeth, made by the family dentist, had shivered to atoms before the resistance of a concrete army biscuit, and he was detained for attention at the dental clinic. In due course a formidable denture was supplied, and its fit tested in the long low hut, with its line of chairs arranged like a barber's saloon.

HAVRE

The eye tooth was too long, and grated on the lower set. Three times the army dentist ground it down and thrust it into Lambert's mouth without obtaining the necessary adjustment. Evidently his patience was not equal to a fourth effort, as ramming the denture home, he growled forcibly :

" I tell you those teeth fit ! Clear out."

The eye tooth broke off at the first meal, but Lambert lacked the courage to make further protest and endured the added discomfort as patiently as his temperament would allow.

With Evans, a giant Welsh bank manager, Thoroughgood, a little workhouse master from Wiltshire, Bright, a versatile chemist, artist and singer, and many other good fellows, he tried to forget the unhappy present and the unknown future.

With them he slept in the hard, rat-ridden tent, ate, argued or gambled; and shared with them a thousand jobs that a soldier must do.

They helped immensely to soften the blow that Fate had dealt him, but nothing compensated for the loss of Home and he almost welcomed the command when it came at last :

A.A. call for H.A.C. Parade full marching order at four o'clock.

The battalion had gaps—terrible gaps after the Bullecourt horrors, and every man was wanted to fill them.

CHAPTER III

QUELMES

It was a queer experience to join suddenly a thousand strangers and yet there was an atmosphere of friendliness that was refreshing after the barely disguised hostility of the base ! Every man or boy smiled kindly and did his little most to make room in an overcrowded barn, found food from the barely sufficient rations, and directed the dusty recruits to washing and drinking water (strictly differentiated throughout the campaign) and paid all the unselfish attentions that mean so much to a stranger.

Lambert and the rest of Draft 24 felt like new boys at a jolly school. A terrific roar filled the barn, men howled at one another ; missiles hurtled through the air. Lumps of bread and cheese, jams and tins of " bully " were dotted all over the place and the walls were confused masses of equipment and rifles. The language was strong, but filtered, and lacked that constant, absurd, and painful reiteration of one word that had torn Lambert's nerves to shreds at Havre.

Many of these men had been through hell at Bullecourt, but when Lambert tried to induce them to talk of their adventures, he failed to extract more than a few careless phrases.

They were a wonderful lot of fellows and Lambert became friendly in time with a number of brothers of famous men. The families of Alfred Noyes, the poet ; Albert Sammons, the violinist ; Rafael Sabatini, the novelist, had all contributed members to the battalion.

QUELMES

There was one amusing meeting. One of the privates had been Editor of *Answers* during the time when Lambert held a position in the same firm. The two men had worked in the same building but could not recognise one another. Photographs were produced, the one of a man with flowing tie and long hair and the other attired in the quiet orderliness of the English business man, and recognition was mutual immediately.

Draft 24 ceased from that noisy hour and merged into the 2nd Batt. H.A.C. They came at an unfortunate time; long treks were commencing and they promptly experienced the torture that is called "movement of troops."

For hour upon hour during the next days the long column moved forward. In fifty minute stretches it trudged up hill and down dale and never were minutes so leaden. Sixty pounds needs lifting at all, but to carry it on one's shoulders for successive hours is almost indescribable. The leather straps cut into shoulders, the pack brings on an intolerable backache that never really disappears, the haversack on one side and the water bottle on the other, rub the skin from thighs, and the rifle gets weightier every mile.

A horrible feature of marching is the sense of slavery —being one of a gang working in the galleys. Whatever the weather, conditions of the roads or men, the Army orders rests every fifty minutes at precisely ten minutes to the hour and until that ardently desired moment the troops must march.

A delay at starting on the last day meant the troops keeping their packs on for nearly two hours, and one of the companies kept up a continuous howl for a rest. A few words from Colonel to Company Commander, and the whole crowd got an hour's pack drill the next evening.

Lambert and Thoroughgood were together and chatted of their new experiences for the first hour, but the conversation died away. The former tried to interest himself in the broad expanse of hedgeless country that spread on each side ; switched his thoughts to home when scenery palled ; forgot all about them when his foot jarred on a stone ; counted paces until he got sick of it ; determined not to look at his watch for half an hour but succumbed after nine and a half minutes, and then groaned when the dial showed another twenty minutes to the next halt.

He noticed Thoroughgood's increasing pallor and complete abandon at the next halt, and made a sympathetic inquiry. The little man did not answer but struggled gamely into his load when command for " packs on " ran down the line.

The battalion were limp, footsore and exhausted when they reached a mile-long hill ending at Quelmes. At the bottom, astride a nice horse, sat the Colonel, a small fluffy-haired man with cold eyes. He surveyed each line of fours with a look reminiscent of a cattle valuer.

" Another half mile," he mentioned at intervals.

The time for another halt occurred midway up the hill and the men hurried to the other side of the road. Lambert saw Thoroughgood stagger, and tried to grasp him, but the little man had fallen with a crash. His pack was taken off him, stretcher-bearers hurried up to open his tunic and dab his face, but when the column moved on to its resting-place, Thoroughgood was still unconscious.

An hour later, when each company were billeted in separate barns, all as foul and dark as one another, he was led in, white and shaky, and laid down beside Lambert, who had only sufficient strength left to turn his head.

" How do you feel, old man," he murmured.

" Pretty rotten. Orderly room to-morrow ! "

Next morning the men who had fallen out were informed that they needed marching practice,

QUELMES

and ordered an hour's pack drill each day for a week. Thoroughgood mentioned the sentence listlessly to Lambert and seemed only mildly interested when that worthy, who at that time found swearing difficult, burst into a passionate torrent of foul language.

Intensive training is a great game if you are physically fit and the weather is dry. Lambert and the evergrowing crowd of " pals " played it for weeks. It needs something larger than a tennis court. Battalions usually play it alone, frequently a brigade indulges and occasionally a division.

You want room to play a game with any number of players up to thirty thousand, and the battalion marched several miles each day to the ground selected. On brilliant September mornings, lines of white flags moved slowly across fields of grass, swedes, or corn. Behind them moved " blobs " of men, bayonets glistening in the sun. Here and there haycocks or sheds flew blue flags. Whistles blew and men moved. The advanced parties kept within distance of the white flags, throwing down any blue that came in their path. Scattered bodies chased about with " shouts " and " whoops," stabbing clods of earth or unoffending turnips. Men squatted down near the blue flags with sighs of content, echoed here and there by others marked down as " casualties."

It was a great game! The white flags represented an artillery barrage; the blue, enemy " pill-boxes," captured by walking over them, and garrisoned later. The " whoopers " were " mopping-up."

One bright morning Lambert was a " casualty," and sitting contentedly beneath a haystack, when an officer, sitting erect on a magnificent horse, galloped into the near distance, followed by a Lancer, upholding a lance bearing a small Union Jack as a pendant.

It was the Commander-in-Chief, Sir Douglas Haig, and a curious tingling ran down Lambert's spine.

He was practically out of the world of news, but others had played that game on those fields, and the remnants were now in the thick of the slaughter, misnamed the Battles of the Ridges.

But the troops knew little of these horrors, and after the day's training there were howls of laughter at night, in the estaminet with the famous " Round Table." The place rocked with laughter or reverberated with beautiful choruses. Occasionally wonderful concerts took place on an old farm wagon, with fine signing by Adams and Walker; marvellous playing by Symons; clever turns by Bennett or Hooper, and fascinating reciting by Farnell.

There were exciting football matches several times a week, and a spirit of reckless happiness pervaded the atmosphere, with a complete indifference to the significance of each day's training.

It was a great game, but the Devil was the most amused. He rocked with laughter and pointed round the table with his long fingers. Singers, footballers and laughter-makers went down like ninepins later, and many a man of that jolly company went to his Eternal Home before the game came to an end.

CHAPTER IV

ZILLEBEKE

ZILLEBEKE was a pleasure trip for the good people of Ypres until July 1914. After that fateful month its pleasures declined rapidly, and it became unhealthy long before a concentration of German artillery smashed all the buildings over a certain height, and made "mice holes" in the lower parts.

It was a nasty mess of wood and bricks as the battalion marched wearily through. Off the main street Lumsden caught a glimpse of the church smashed almost beyond recognition. On the side of a terrible hovel hung the red triangle of the Y.M.C.A., and a little lower down, the plain enamelled sign of the Church Army—two oases in a desert of ruin—while here and there men watched from the sandbagged holes in which they evidently existed.

To many of the men dragging along under their loads, Zillebeke was the first sight of war's work, and it struck them very forcibly, but later they were to look on it as quite a healthy resort, where a riotous hour could be spent, drinking hot tea out of condensed milk tins in a cellar, splendidly illuminated by two carefully shaded candles. At present, however, it was a dreadful reminder of War; the wreckage left on the beach after the tide had subsided. Full-tide was a few miles farther, in the direction of the Ypres salient, from which came that muffled roar that sounded like fifty distant zoos.

Packs were dumped at a camp a foot deep in mud,

and the troops altered their equipment to battle order, and prepared to rest their weary limbs on the muddy floors of their tents. They moved forward again next day, nearer to that roar, passing on the way several dead mules who had evidently died some years before.

Dusk was deepening into night as they neared a large sheet of water, and there was little noise beyond the tramping of feet, and that omnipresent rumble. Suddenly away on the right there was a terrific crash, followed by a blinding glare. Heads jerked up suddenly from their droop, hands gripped rifles, but the steady tramp proceeded without a hitch. Some well-informed person told all and sundry that the noise proceeded from a fifteen-inch naval gun, truck-mounted, and running wherever rails could be laid.

A few minutes later Lambert heard the powerful hum of an aeroplane. It sounded near, and the next instant there was a splitting roar in an adjacent field, then a rush of wind, another crash, and he found himself in the ditch. Most of the platoon were with him.

"That's the stuff to give 'em," said the platoon officer, thinking of the big gun. A glance round and he found that all his men had disappeared.

"What the hell are you up to?" he shouted, "out of it. On the road. What in . . ."

"We've been bombed, sir," said an aggrieved voice. "There are some men hit."

The casualties were left in the charge of stretcher-bearers and the battalion moved on, the recruits "blooded." The man walking on Lambert's left was missing, a decent sized lump of bomb had put his ankle out of gear permanently. Thoroughgood was on the right and walked a hundred yards without comment.

"Look at my rifle, Lambo," he said quietly.

For a foot from the muzzle the woodwork had disappeared. Some sharp splinter had cut through it as clean as a whistle, and the rifle had been slung two inches from the little man's head. Lambert's half-patronising, half-contemptuous liking for a smaller, less robust man deepened suddenly into admiration and envy.

The battalion rested for the night in a magnificent dug-out on the banks of Zillebeke Lake. Cut in the side of a railway embankment, it extended for a long distance, with paths and rooms and hundreds of wire mattresses in tiers.

Lambert slept quite well that night. After a month or two of hard ground, the yielding wires were an immense relief to his aching legs and sore joints. At dawn a thunderous roar aroused him, then another, which shook the huge cavern from end to end. He slipped quietly to the entrance, and was flung backwards by a powerful draught of wind.

Framed in the entrance was a picture he never forgot.

From all sides darted flashes of brilliant fire, a perfect aurora of flame, silhouetting squat bushes, shattered tree trunks and pock-marked fields gleaming with water. In the sky gleamed dozens of brilliant blue lights, varied by showers of lovely golden balls, while in the higher air there was a continuous drone of planes, and frequent explosions that shook the world.

Lambert saw the fireworks, the brilliant gun flashes from an enormous circle, the sudden glares of shells bursting in our territory, but all appeared to fire or explode without individual noise. All sound merged into a continuous ear-splitting roar that dulled his brain, and he could only pick out the occasional, inimitable thunder of the 15-inch naval gun firing from the railway above. The composite effect was lovely, awful, wonderful and terrifying.

He caught a glimpse of another watcher,

"Somethin' doin'," he murmured, hoping that his voice was calm. It did not matter what he said. The keenest ear could not have picked up a full-throated shout from a hundred men. The roar and blinding flashes continued for minutes, dying down at intervals to bearable proportions, then rising again in a crescendo of nerve-shattering vibrations until Lambert covered his ears and staggered back into the recesses of the dug-out.

The British were attacking once again, and several thousand muddy and exhausted Prussians dragged along the road in the chilly dawn.

CHAPTER V

"AMMUNITION AND DUCK-BOARDS"

Two hundred men were wanted the next afternoon. As they formed up, Thoroughgood subsided into a heap. The strain of long marches, the narrow escape from the bomb, and the present nerve tension had been too much for the little man, who had fainted. They carried him to the aid post and administered a restorative and led him back a few minutes later, white and sick.

What the job was, Lambert knew not. It was veiled in the secrecy so common in the Army, and galling in the extreme to men with the average allotment of brain, but he determined to keep as near to his pal as possible, if their work took them through hell itself.

The route lay through damp fields, dotted everywhere with huge gun-pits. Under the screens of green camouflage nets squatted hundreds of great howitzers, mostly covered with tarpaulin of splotchy colours to hide them from the continuous reconnaissance of enemy planes.

On a rough road stood an "Archie"; its crew posed as though for a photograph, with an officer peering through strong glasses at distant specks. A short order, repeated in the monotone of long habit, and the wicked, green- and black-slashed barrel deflected. Another order, with its echo; the clanging opening of a door, the insertion of a shell and the gun fired with a shattering crash. A blob of smoke appeared ten thousand feet up and floated lazily away, well under the black specks, which appeared and disappeared in dozens every few minutes.

The track merged into a road made of timber baulks, splintered and broken in places, gone altogether elsewhere. On each side was the débris of years. Broken bricks and lumps of masonry, remains of lorries, broken tree trunks, shells of all sizes, rusty coils of wire, pieces of leather equipment, ancient tin hats, skulls of dead animals and here and there graves, the inscriptions on the crosses dull and indistinct.

A dreadful smell pervaded the atmosphere. The odour of rotting wood, decaying flesh and poisoned earth combined with the sickly smell of cordite and high explosive. The most dreadful atmosphere known to man floated over the salient, the charnel-house of Europe.

Shell holes were everywhere, and Lambert noticed with a sense of chill that water stood in them at a foot's depth, although there had been little rain for a fortnight.

The party struck the Menin Road, lined with high stacks of every kind of war material and crowded with every conceivable kind of traffic, that split the party into small bodies very effectively. A few hundred yards of spasmodic marching, and the men fell out on the side of the road. It was not a pleasant spot, and Lambert interrogated a corporal who joined them.

" Got to take 100,000 rounds of S.A.A. to Brigade Headquarters. Jerry is counter-attacking to-night ! "

" Thanks for those few nuts," returned Lambert.

In his turn, a few minutes later, he seized one end of a box containing a thousand cartridges and Thoroughgood seized the other. The little man's face had a sickly pallor but he seized his end of the eighty-pound load without a word.

The men, burdened with battle order, started across the most awful country conceivable. One side of

"AMMUNITION AND DUCK-BOARDS"

the road was the result of Ancient History; the other was modern, painfully, horribly recent. As far as the eye could see stretched desolate fields, and not a yard of their surface was free of its shell hole. Every scrap of trees, fences, houses, civilisation in fact, had disappeared, blown into atoms. In their places were holes, reeking evilly of powder, in which muddy water oozed.

Slipping and sliding, the H.A.C. were guided slowly along. The only indications of any track were roughly painted boards, bearing a hand pointing to the horror and proclaiming "Brigade X." In the distance, atop a slight rise, rested a huge, deserted tank.

Fifty yards on a good road is quite far enough for a box of "ammo." That distance on a week-old battlefield is like ten miles. Men slid all over the place. First one foot went down, then the other. Frequently falls were complete and man and box came down with a crash. Every few yards the bearers adopted a change of method, and excellent friends quarrelled violently on behalf of their respective opinions.

Down from the head of the line came admonitions, from the rear encouragement, and vice versa. Breathing came short and husky with the exertion, and though the gathering dusk brought a chill with it, there were beads of perspiration on every man's brow. A man had fallen into a hole full of treacherous mud and four men were needed to extract him, like a cork from a bottle.

Lambert was breathing in short gasps. The box was getting heavier at every step, and the muscles of his arms ached abominably. Times without number he had slipped and staggered, and on each occasion the jar shocked every nerve. Thoroughgood plodded on, his head and shoulders arched to such an extent that it was hard to see his face.

Suddenly there came a low murmur. Then a whine, and away on the left a metallic crash and a high shower of mud and stones. Another followed in quick succession, then a third and fourth.

The procession halted momentarily and then kept on. Lambert felt his breath stop and the sense of hearing seemed to leap to its acutest point. Another whine, louder this time, and a shell burst a hundred yards nearer. It was followed by its mates. A still louder noise, almost a scream, and his senses jumbled into a tangled mass.

"Body of Christ! Save me!" flashed through his mind, and instinctively he threw himself headlong on the ground. The same instant everything seemed to blow up, a torrent of earth and muck shot at him with considerable force, rattling on his tin hat and filling his mouth, eyes and nose. Scarcely believing himself alive, he got to his knees with an insane desire to laugh.

"Where did that one go to, Erb?" he gurgled foolishly. "Are you—are you hurt, old boy?"

"No," came the faint response, and Thoroughgood scrambled to his feet.

Halts were frequent now. Shells rained on every side, several men lay in the mud with stretcher-bearers binding their wounds, and the shock seemed to have deprived the others of their vitality.

They rested at the bottom of the only rise to be seen, while the air vibrated with the crashing explosion of high explosive shells. Time and again every man lay flat on his face as one came perilously near. As the order was passed along to re-start, a shell burst at the top of the ridge and a lump of jagged metal, large enough to cut them in two, whizzed by Thoroughgood's body and buried itself in the ground near Lambert's head. Neither said a word and God alone knows what they said in their hearts.

At the top of the ridge stood a tank, a nasty jagged

"AMMUNITION AND DUCK-BOARDS" 45

hole in the side telling a tragic story. A few yards away lay the body of an Australian, his calm dead face gleaming a dull yellow.

Polygon Wood, the scene of desperate fighting, *had* started on the other side of that ridge, but all traces of it had disappeared. There was not a shred of it left. Not only had the trees been blown down, but every trunk had been blasted to atoms, and every leaf and blade of grass buried beneath tons of mud. Except for deserted pill-boxes just visible in the gloom the vista was of utter desolation, a nightmare picture of muddy shell holes.

The fatigue party staggered through this ghastly spot, shaking with tension and physical fatigue. Shells burst everywhere and men ducked their heads, or dropped their boxes time after time. The N.C.O.'s were splendid.

"Keep on, boys," they shouted repeatedly. "*That's* a long way off. Keep going! Soon be there."

An officer came along and took Thoroughgood's place, and Lambert was so fatigued that he scarcely noticed the change. Another age—long ten minutes—and he felt the box drag heavily in the mud. With tired eyes he slowly turned his head and found another assistant, a red-haired boy with blue eyes. His head was sagging from side to side and he was crying bitterly. All his strength had gone and perforce his end trailed along the ground. Another of those dreadful screams, and Lambert rose from his crouching position to find the boy lying beside him in a welter of blood.

"Sorry, Lambo," he whispered; "I'm beastly tired. Nasty headache."

Stretcher-bearers—heroes to a man on that and every other occasion—hurried up and took charge of the wounded boy, while another seized the rope handle of the box.

"Come along, sonny. Another hundred yards!"

he said, and the fact that he was fifteen years the junior did not matter. Lambert went, but his strength was gone.

" I can't, I'm done ! Let me die ! " he panted.

" All right, sonny ! Go and die in that shell hole ! "

Lambert subsided into a heap on its muddy side and panted horribly, while his companion calmly watched the shells bursting. He allowed a few minutes to elapse and then induced Lambert to make an effort, and that worthy used his last ounce of strength in depositing his burden in the large hole dug within easy distance of " The Mound," a large rifle butt, now full of dug-outs, and used as Brigade Headquarters.

Lambert staggered, rather than walked, on the return journey. Limbs were shaking and aching, his head was swimming, and through his brain ran a jumble of prayers and curses, thoughts of home, and unending questions that half framed themselves and then faded into foolish meaningness.

Shells burst everywhere, but he no longer cared or troubled to stop and duck. Physical endurance seemed to have reached its limits, and he hoped that one would hit him and end the misery.

Happening to glance round, he noticed a red light shoot into the sky, followed by a white and a yellow. In an instant a huge semi-circle of fire blazed in front of him, and the greatest concatenation of sound he had ever conceived burst upon his ears. Words fail to describe the incredible pandemonium. It was hellish ! Ten thousand raging, devastating thunderstorms rolled into one was only an approximation of that appalling outburst.

Personal feeling died before that earth-shattering storm of man-killing metal. The private stumbled on, unconscious of energy, his mind unable to recognise that the continuous whines overhead were shells leaving, not coming. He did not know that he was

"AMMUNITION AND DUCK-BOARDS" 47

completely exhausted until he fell on his wire mattress in Railway Embankment, fully dressed, and slept like a log.

Many men were killed and wounded on that trip to "The Mound," but "Jerry" had counter-attacked in force and had only been beaten back by that colossal barrage and the wonderful firing of the front-line troops, who had wanted those 100,000 rounds.

The Brigadier-General congratulated the H.A.C. on their fine work in not "losing" a box. He knew those shell holes, and was not unaware of the fact that the enemy had the track "taped" to an inch, and shelled it continuously.

The demands of modern war are insatiable, and several hundred men from the H.A.C. and Manchesters had to make that little trip again a day or two later. This time each man carried a "duck-board," stout boards strongly nailed to thick baulks of timber.

To balance them and walk along the treacherous track was a feat in itself: the weight was so great that all desire for life died before the journey was a quarter over, but perhaps because of that fact the inevitable "strafe" lost much of its effect and the brave boys kept going as though shells were rain drops.

Engineers superintended the work, and a wonderful duck-board track grew slowly over that dreadful morass. There were many more casualties, but the journey to "The Mound" was never so terrible afterwards, and the work was immortalised by a picture in a daily picture paper. It showed six men walking in a fog and was as much like the real thing as an elephant resembles a butterfly.

A cinematograph picture by the finest camera in the world would not have done justice to the energies of the British Army during those days. Field guns had been dragged over a mile of that clogging mud; swarms of men were laying railway lines upon which would run enormous pieces of artillery, and all the time enemy shells burst round and among them. Lambert felt a glow of pride run through his weary heart. This army could never be beaten, unless they all died !

Staggering "home," with every limb aching and head drooping with complete exhaustion, he heard the whistle of a shell. Dimly he realised that it was very near but he was too indifferent to alter his movements. The next second and there was a colossal explosion, and a fountain of smoke fifty feet high mounted to the heavens in front of him.

He stopped dead, fell flat, got up again, ran forward and then back as though the fiend were after him. Earth and stones hit him, and rattled on his tin hat like rain; great clods of clay pounded into the earth on either side, and all kinds of débris rained down for several minutes before clear thinking returned and he felt fit to resume the journey.

A battery of 18-pounders had been brought up, and " Jerry " had hit the ammunition dump. Where the guns had been there was a hole twenty feet deep. Men were already digging to try and save buried gunners, and a hundred yards away Lambert walked mournfully past the covered body of a friend, killed at that distance by a flying piece of shell.

CHAPTER VI

"JOLTING HORSE" TRENCH

LIVING in the abomination of desolation (to say nothing of sudden death and terrible wounds; mud, rain and privation) would have been more bearable if news from home had been good, but each man with the susceptibility of a maggot, felt, when he read his letters, that the cup was near to overflowing.

The German airmen were killing women and children in England. Their foul work was going on frequently and regularly, and the bravest heart among those wonderful women could scarcely conceal the growing anxiety of each moonlit night, or repress entirely details of the bloody war fiends waged upon the infant and the aged.

Many square miles of the Ypres sector were covered with ammunition of all kinds, and not a night passed without a succession of air raids. "Archies" were firing continuously, there was an incessant whirr of planes in the air: squadron after squadron dropped bombs until the earth trembled, men died, or valuable property was blown to atoms. Sixty raiders was an ordinary night's total, while in the daylight hundreds of machines flew in little bunches, and the air was full of white or black "blobs" that floated away lazily before the wind.

It was part of the necessary endurance for the fighters, but the thought of their women-folk, parents and little ones suffering the same mental torture drove them frantic. . . . The German High Command possibly desired moral effect. They got it.

In the midst of terrible danger, when shells rained through the air and showers of bullets sang songs, Britishers thought of graceful women and curly-haired babies blown to atoms, and hung on by their back teeth, or " went into them " like Red Indians, fanatical and thirsting for the blood of their enemies.

All the men felt an approximation of this lust as they set out on their third journey along their " Via Dolorosa." Ninety per cent of them knew nothing of the work to be done, but the crushing load each carried suggested serious business. In addition to the usual battle order, full complement of ammunition and gas masks, there were many Lewis guns, bomb-bags crowded with Mills' bombs, Hale's grenades, smoke bombs, S.O.S. rockets, and all the regalia of an attacking force to be humped, and each man resembled a pack mule.

They set out heavily weighted, not only with foreboding, but solid metal, and how war correspondents could have talked of troops marching cheerfully to battle is beyond a soldier's imagination.

They plodded manfully along a new timber track, keeping on when nature told them to stop ; helping one another along as much as possible ; giving warning of broken holes or timbers dug by shells, and every man assisting the other to " get there " somehow, anyhow.

They shared the track with ponies and mules carrying shells to the forward guns ; a wonderful procession that seemed unending, ridden by tin-hatted R.F.A. men with eyes wide open for pitfalls ; and animals picking their steps on the broken track with wonderful precision.

The guns were quiet for the first hour or so, and Lambert, between gasps, had murmured that " Jerry " was having his tea when a quartette of shells whinnied over and burst a short distance away. Then began the usual " strafe," but familiarity breeds resignation in war (not contempt, with showers of 5.9s !) and the

"JOLTING HORSE" TRENCH

column kept on steadily. The ammunition ponies had evidently "delivered the goods," for they commenced the return journey. Lambert felt his breath stop as the first of them passed him. With cocked ears, distended nostrils, and hoarse breathing, the little animal pounded over the track like a thing possessed, its rider crouching over its neck like a Yankee jockey. Close at its heels came another, and nose to tail the animals thundered over the timber at an astonishing pace. They jumped holes and large splinters of wood, rushed giddily down slippery slopes and charged up inclines, poured in a line through the smoke of exploded shells, and disappeared into the distance like an overdue express. Those beasts knew the Ypres salient !

Their route led past the ill-omened "Mound," skirted a hole full of dead men and led into a deep trench cut in the mud. They relieved a regiment of the Devons, who resembled a collection of men in an advanced stage of petrification. Every face was stone grey, with staring eyes and chattering teeth. In the narrowness of the trench it was inevitable that the H.A.C. should crash into their fellows as they struggled along to their positions.

Men collided violently, rifles hit bodies or tin hats, toes were trodden into the mud, but not a curse or expostulation came from the Devons, who seemed too dazed or frozen with cold or horror to understand that their relief had actually arrived.

For some unknown reason the trench was called "Jolting Horse," and Lambert could only surmise that the reverberations of the earth during the incessant "strafing" had been the reason. It was the "support" trench and the enemy knew it. He had had it once and his shooting was as accurate as the margin of error would allow. Drizzling rain fell throughout the night, and the men sat low down in the earth, their ground-sheets round their shoulders, or over their tin hats, listening and waiting for what might be.

Shells crashed everywhere. Thin points of light flashed in the background. The air was full of whines and shrieks, interspersed with roars, and over everything floated a pall of smoke, reeking of powder and *poisoned dust.*

Showers of earth and stone fell incessantly; at frequent intervals a considerable portion of the trench fell in completely, or partially, burying the men beneath, necessitating immediate digging in the first case, and a desperate spluttering heave of the shoulders in the other. A thunderous roar, flash of flame, and a reek of cordite told of direct hits, and whispers would pass along the trench from each end, converging on the men nearest the blue-back hole that marred its symmetry.

" Who's hit ? Who's hit ? Who's hit ? "

Sometimes the answer came back, sometimes it did not. Men who had escaped death by some miraculous decree of Providence could hardly feel, and found speech impossible with their bodies and clothes spattered with the blood of their friends. Men disappeared that night absolutely and utterly. Others could be seen when daylight came—lying quietly, yards outside the trench.

Lambert was at the extreme end of the trench, and throughout the night, and the next day, a procession of men passed him on the way to the aid post at " The Mount." All kinds of men and boys, with all kinds of wounds. Some holding arms tightly, their teeth clenched and faces working; some holding their heads and moaning with intolerable pain ; others smiling in a ghastly semi-insane condition. During the night, and early dawn, men carried or escorted the poor fellows to the aid post, but at frequent intervals during the night Lambert was surrounded by a dreadful gathering of wounded, unable to face the storm of shells.

Daylight brought fresh terrors. As soon as the light got strong, enemy snipers fired at the slightest target and the uninjured men heard with horror

"JOLTING HORSE" TRENCH

that crack and "ping," as their chums made the dangerous journey.

Nobody moved about in daylight with impunity. Stretcher-bearers, whose names should be set in diamonds on some immortal memorial, went out, time after time, trying to bring back "stretcher cases" from the battalion who had attacked near Passchendaele Ridge.

They crossed shell-swept "No Man's Land" on their errand of mercy, and always the enemy fired on them, although their telescopic sights must have shown them the work in progress. Shots followed them from start to finish, and for coldly calculated bravery their persistence was hard to beat, even in a war teeming with heroism.

As soon as a man was hit, a "reserve" took his place, and many a poor devil, racked with agony, had cause to bless the "base-wallahs," and did so fervently.

Lambert peered cautiously over the parapet as one party returned with its burden. Bullets spattered right and left, behind and in front, but the heroes kept on steadily and lowered their stretcher carefully into the trench. Another crack, a moan of pain, and one of the carriers held a bleeding wrist high in the air, and then fell headlong. Lambert ground his teeth, and swore furiously in a paroxysm of rage that produced a faint smile from Thoroughgood, sitting quietly a hundred yards away.

Hours passed on leaden wings and the men sat patiently in the mud waiting for night, almost oblivious of the drizzle, or the infernal shower of shells that scarcely ceased. They ate and drank little, although a fatigue party had lost many men bringing up rations through the enemy barrage. The bread was sodden and broken, but many lives had been lost bringing it. Some hours after darkness had fallen a whisper ran along the line:

"*Prepare to move!*"

CHAPTER VII

BROODSEINDE RIDGE

A TAPE had been run from " supports " to the " jumping-off " line. It guided the companies who were to attack over dank fields, dotted with low bushes and innumerable shell holes, down a slope to a foul swamp deep in treacherous mud, which had to be crossed carefully, in single file, to avoid a muddy death.

Shells burst in the middle of the regiment as the various sections were bundled into position. Officers and sergeants shouted and pushed, sections collided in the pitch darkness; were posted here and there, and eventually reached a third point, and all seemed confusion, with ghastly death grinning overhead.

It was about the hour when the human frame is dubbed at its weakest when the various platoons found their places, and huddled together in shallow trenches a foot deep in the mud. For the first time in those long days of horror a definite statement was given to " the men." It was definite enough at last !

"*We attack this morning. Our barrage opens at 3.50 !*"

There was no mention of objective. So far as Lambert knew they had to go on until killed, captured, or were marching on the long road to Germany; but this lack of orders did not worry him at the moment. His mind was full of a confused mixture of thoughts of home, prayers for strength and a queer sympathy for his comrades, sitting so motionless in the muddy pools.

BROODSEINDE RIDGE

Now and again he murmured a few words to the man next him, a fat, jolly-faced Londoner, brimming with good humour; but a shock ran through him as he caught a glimpse of his friend's face in the red glare of an explosion. The round cheeks had fallen in; deep lines were graven on the freckled face, and all the merry twinkle had disappeared from the staring eyes.

"Buck up, old dear! It'll be all right!"

"No! No! This ends it. My-my poor girl. We love one another so much. We were going to be married during my leave. Now . . ."

His voice trailed away into nothingness and Lambert could say no more. For the first time he saw the look, and heard the voice, of one of those men who knew definitely that their last day had come. It became a familiar, unexplainable phenomenon, but the first instance shocked him into silence. He sat stock still, wondering dully if this was his last day also.

Just before 3.50 the men crawled out of the mud and walked leisurely to their positions. An unnatural stillness had fallen over everything, prolonging seconds into illimitable measures of time, and eternities passed as Lambert knelt on the mud, peering into the dark.

A series of screams through the air and hell broke loose. With a swift sweep of the arm, the platoon officer pointed to the dark void ahead. Up jumped the long line and into pandemonium they ran. Straight forward into a world afire, shaking with appalling crashes of high explosives; the metallic explosions of overhead shrapnel; the deadly song of concentrated machine guns.

Men toppled over immediately. The symmetrical line became jagged. The platoon officer disappeared; the section commander dropped heavily and rolled over, motioning onwards as he lay. The platoon sergeant was nowhere to be seen and only one thought occurred to Lambert: "Get on!"

The greatest concentration of enemy artillery that the glorious 7th Division had ever experienced in their long record of terrible fighting had dropped upon them at the instant that the British drumfire had opened. Lots were killed. Officers and N.C.O.'s had gone. They must go on. No use going back. The world was mad.

"You're in charge, Ross," he howled excitedly, as he ran and stumbled over the broken earth and through the clinging mud.

Ross turned and grinned, and Lambert remembered him standing on the fire-step in " Jolting Horse " Trench calmly watching shells burst almost in his face. This was the man to lead!

Up a long field the remainder of the section charged, tripping and jumping over barbed wire and poor motionless bodies; taking no notice of the bullets that whined unceasingly around them, or the jagged fragments of iron that crashed around them like giant hailstones.

Into a narrow trench, lying just under the top of a ridge, they bundled, and over the top like a pack of hounds. In the feeble rays of the early dawn appeared the enemy line. It ran at right angles round the village of Reutel, one arm running down the slope, another cutting away to their left. Some yards behind the trenches was a pill-box: a squat square of white concrete, spitting out bullets in an unending stream. Right away on the left, more spurts of flame and several dark figures in a crouching position.

Down on their knees went Ross and several other men and headlong into a deep shell hole went Lambert. In a second all their rifles cracked out, and almost simultaneously with the disappearance of the machine gun team, Ross, and those nearest him, crumpled into a terribly intermingled heap.

There was too much noise, too much mental excite-

BROODSEINDE RIDGE

ment to feel sorrow at that minute; the mind simply contained a jumble of thoughts. The enemy in sight had disappeared. Who else was there to kill? Ha! there goes one. Crack! God have mercy! Am I alive? Another clip! Crack! Crack! Don't fire across my ear, you blasted fool!

A Lewis gun crashed out from a hole a few yards to the right, spraying the German trench and pill-box with a terrific stream of bullets. Great shells from the British guns were sending buildings in Becelare high in the air; the dreadful line of the German barrage had followed the attackers and was now bursting behind the ridge.

Suddenly the fire from the pill-box ceased, and a shout from the next shell hole just reached Lambert's ears. He turned and saw a sergeant looking in his direction.

"Fire at that trench," came faintly through the uproar. He turned and nodded, and saw with a feeling of sickness the tin hat jump violently off the man's head, and the immediate fading of life as a bullet crashed through the brain.

Mechanically he fired bullet after bullet at the dun line that wound down the slope, until his rifle smoked and was too hot to hold longer. Twisting on his side, his feet slid down the muddy bank, and he sat suddenly in a pool of water that oozed and bubbled at the bottom. The chill seemed to steady him, and he glanced cautiously round to take his bearings.

Evidently the ridge had been captured, for no firing came from the enemy trench or pill-box. To right and left he could see the tops of tin helmets peeping over the edges of shell holes. The Lewis gun was silent; its muzzle smoking and its ammunition drums empty. Everywhere his comrades were lying in all attitudes, many perfectly still, others writhing in pain. For the first time, Lambert realised that he had companions, a boy whose facial formation resulted in a fixed grin that was annoying in such circumstances and who had fired right across his face, and a comrade from the same platoon. All the other jolly boys! Where were they? That straight line that had pressed forward so manfully! Had it dwindled so dreadfully? Lambert did not dare to answer the questions even to himself.

"What do we do now?" he asked irritably, and scrambled into an upright position. For answer a bullet whizzed into the earth behind him; and now the roar of artillery had subsided, there came the continuous cracking of snipers' rifles. Many a man survived the attack that day only to get a bullet through his head. The sniping was fiendish—an inch above the ground level was sufficient excuse for the immediate crack of a rifle.

Inaction is dreadful in times of peace, but add the discomfort of crouching, or lying, in sticky mud, with legs up to the knees in a pool of water, and the result is unbearable. After enduring the discomfort for a couple of hours, Lambert offered to reconnoitre, but a corporal bravely essayed the task of recrossing the ridge in an endeavour to discover the next move.

He crawled rapidly on hands and knees over the undulating shell holes, gathered himself into a crouching position and dashed, head well down, for the top. A clever swerve probably saved him, for a bullet practically touched him, but he was over the top before the next came.

An hour later Lambert happened to notice a head peep cautiously over the edge of the ridge, and a finger beckoned to him. He passed the word along to his companions, and one by one they made the dangerous trip. Each man ran or crawled over the muddy flats, plunging down slippery sides of holes, and scrambling up the others, and gradually working nearer the top, ending up with a frantic rush as the inevitable bullet zipped perilously near them.

BROODSEINDE RIDGE

One of the Lewis gun team dragged the heavy gun behind him and paused for a second on the skyline to pull it after him. A bullet went clean through his wrist, but the brave fellow persisted and that gun was one of the few that survived that awful day.

Lambert felt a gambler's thrill as his turn came, but Providence was preserving him, and he tumbled safely into the trench that so many poor boys had rushed through hours before.

It was full of wounded men, and Lambert sickened as he crawled by white-faced, bleeding comrades to where his platoon sergeant, a taciturn uncouth young man, sat in a "cubby-hole" scraped in the side. His offer to do anything possible was answered by a nod and he set about making himself useful.

A "cubby-hole" for a poor fellow wounded in the head; a waterproof wrapped round another who was shivering with cold, a rough bandage round a wounded arm and a careful watch at a gap under observation by the enemy, helped to keep his mind off the horrors.

A few men crawled in during the day, and Lambert was overjoyed when Thoroughgood joined him unhurt. The little man brought news of many chums, and it was a terrible tale. Dozens of mutual friends killed, many more wounded. Not a single officer untouched. Doctor, Adjutant, Company-Sergeant-Major all killed, Their platoon officer, a popular subaltern, was lying in a shell hole fifty yards away, with a bullet wound in the neck, with men for company who would never obey his orders again. Still farther away lay the Company Commander, grievously wounded by a bullet that had smashed its way into his body, and emerged near the collar-bone.

Few dared to move in the daylight. Shells fell every few seconds and deadly snipers took toll of men who exposed themselves. Heroes defied death dozens of times, and chief among them modest, cheerful, lion-hearted Tantum, R.A.M.C. attached H.A.C. He had followed the battalion against orders, and now darted about the stricken field, despite a nasty hole in his back, bandaging, encouraging or threatening as the case demanded. He had previously won the Military Medal, which he never wore, and afterwards received a bar, when the V.C. was the only fitting decoration.

Daylight slowly faded, and the evening air grew chilly. The little band seemed isolated from the world, and for hours Lambert resigned himself to eventual capture, until a Welsh Fusilier officer and sergeant crawled into the trench, and pointed out the direction to be taken when darkness fell. There was no food or drink for the men, but the reeking fumes of cordite had given them a sickening nausea and no desire for food. The wounded men were languid with pain, lying half-unconscious in all attitudes.

From all around came moans, and an incessant wail from some poor boy, that resembled the lament of a lost soul. For hours it racked their sensitive nerves.

"S-t-r-e-t-c-h-e-r B-e-a-r-e-r H-A-C. Oh! God! Will nobody come? Mother! Oh! Mother."

Lambert writhed in mental agony; the hopelessness of the position hurting him almost beyond endurance. Stretcher-bearers there were none—not one came through unwounded. A rush to some unknown spot in the distance probably meant a bullet, and powerlessness to help if he got through, and alas! there were many men in similar straits. He howled patience at the top of his voice, but the same cry was the only answer.

Lambert lay on his stomach, watching through the gap in the trench as the light failed. Counter-attacks were possible and obviously they would not come in the daylight. A slight sound attracted his attention, and over the top of the shell holes to the left of the trench came his platoon officer.

BROODSEINDE RIDGE

His face was deadly white, a bloody bandage swathed his neck, and his rainproof was soaked with the blood of a sniper's victim. Slowly and painfully he crawled on his hands and knees, stopping every few yards for fresh strength.

It was deadly dangerous ground and the progress was so slow that Lambert expected the crack of a rifle any second. Some hand held back the enemy, and the injured man dragged himself along by inches, while Lambert watched him with fascinated eyes. Right opposite the gap, the officer sank wearily on to his elbows, his head sagging down into the mud, and Lambert's blood ran cold.

" Keep going, sir, for heaven's sake ! They are sniping like hell there. Come on, sir, come on ! "

The urgent appeal had its effect. Slowly and painfully the poor fellow struggled on to his hands and knees, and moving an inch at a time crossed the dangerous gap, to sink exhausted into a muddy " cubby-hole."

He rested for half an hour and then resumed the painful journey to the reserve trenches, and, it being dark, the scanty remnants of a strong attacking force followed soon after.

CHAPTER VIII

GETTING OUT!

No words can describe adequately a British attack, and German defence, in the salient. The operations and number of men were so vast, the successes and failures so intermingled, that an attempt to describe the technical features would be beyond the limited powers of any writer and hopelessly boring to the reader.

Impossible as it is to bring a clear picture of these giant operations before the mind, it is not hard to paint the position of survivors. They had advanced over the enemy ground after losing all officers, and many N.C.O.'s, and captured enemy positions at great cost; "supports" had come up to occupy them and all that remained was the necessity to "get out."

It sounds simple, but several miles of devastated country lay between the new line and the rest "billets," and over this black and blasted expanse of mud and bog swept a tornado of metal.

In addition, the few uninjured men were almost exhausted after lying in mud for over two days, with little food and drink, and enduring the indescribable strain produced by modern artillery. The position of the badly wounded, lying in agony for long hours can be mentioned, but no brain can comprehend it fully.

The Company Commander had to lie in agony for the whole day. Every movement meant terrible pain from the wound, and as the hours passed his

GETTING OUT! 63

limbs grew cramped and cold, and he became delirious at intervals. Several privates were with him and did their utmost to keep him warm, but the wound was too terrible to admit of much relief, and they could only murmur futile words of comfort, or shift him gently when a position became intolerable.

All rank faded into insignificance in the face of suffering almost too great to bear, and the death that might meet them all at any minute. A corporal bandaged his stricken captain as skilfully as possible and shifted him to another position with the gentleness of a woman, while the officer nestled up to him like a poor stricken child. "Get close!" he murmured. "It keeps me warm. I'm cold—cold."

Man after man attempted the dangerous job of trying to find non-existent stretcher-bearers or stretchers, but none of them were able to return, and when darkness fell the remaining corporal, with his commander's arm round his neck, practically carried him inch by inch to the trench occupied by the remnants of the company. Once again efforts were made to find a stretcher, but the search was hopeless, and the poor officer could not lie on a makeshift of puttees wound between rifles.

There was nothing for it but for the corporal to continue his merciful task of carrying the officer to the distant Aid Post, a journey of infinite torture to both. From first to last it took sixteen hours, and the corporal obeying the most necessary order to remove his equipment was later fined sixteen shillings for doing so! This is one instance of hundreds, and there were cases where wounded men lay in their blood for three days before help could reach them.

Meanwhile the survivors shivered through hours of rain, mud and misery. Trembling in every limb, they leaned listlessly against the trench wall too exhausted in mind and body to talk or heed the continual explosions. One of these ended a friendship, so common in the Army—sudden, strengthening daily, and ending in separation and suffering. After the foul fog of chemical fumes had drifted away, Lambert noticed Thoroughgood lying at the bottom of the trench.

"My arm's gone!" he murmured, "my arm's gone!"

"No! No!" his friend replied huskily. "It's a 'Blighty' one. Your arm's still there; stick it, old boy. Hi! Pass the word for a stretcher-bearer!"

A man hurried down the trench and the poor little man was examined, and the crushed shoulder blade tenderly dressed.

Lambert choked as they led him away.

"A 'Blighty' one," he gurgled. "Soon be home with that little woman now. Cheeri-o!"

Hurried consultations took place in the darkness. Every officer had gone on a longer or shorter journey, and the initiative rested with a sergeant and several corporals. They grasped the terrible situation manfully: men were sent to Brigade for instructions and rations, and volunteers were requested to carry down wounded.

A loose-limbed youngster, who showed little sign of the prolonged agony, bravely stood forward and did splendid work during the night, carrying down stretcher cases after shedding his heavy equipment and rifle. His reward did not appear in the *Gazette*, but it is graven in many a memory!

Lambert tried to volunteer but nature rebelled. Every limb was aching and refused to work. A deadly nausea had seized him and waves of sickness swept over him periodically. The days of strain, privation and excessive energy had thoroughly exhausted his older system, and the tin hat on his head seemed to be crushing out all sense.

From a great distance, a voice reached his dulled mind and mechanically he followed along the trench.

Some unknown friend assisted him up the steep steps, and staggering from side to side he followed in the wake of a few men, in little better condition than himself.

They had to find the way in the darkness across "No Man's Land," to "Jolting Horse" Trench. During the attack great fissures had been blown in the tape, and the party wandered about like a rudderless ship. The terrain was devoid of landmarks; no stars or moon were out (fortunately in many respects) and right across the district ran the wide swamp, deep in treacherous mud. The party tried several paths across it, to find them impassable after many men had sunk to their waists. Time after time, plucky fellows waded in and had to be lugged out forcibly, and all the time shells shrieked over them at regular intervals, and machine guns sent streams of bullets sweeping across the ground.

Success rewarded their persistent efforts and the men filed through a swampy path. Half had started when wild shouts for help pierced the darkness. They fell unheeded. The men had borne too much to stop. Again they were howled out, and this time with a personal appeal that could not be disregarded.

"Help! For God's sake," came the shout, ending in a wail. "Are the H.A.C. going to let a fellow drown?"

Half a dozen men stopped and hurried along to the source of the noise. It came from a man in the Durham Light Infantry, buried deep in the mud. He was already up to his chest and only his outstretched arms were saving him from a dreadful death. It took six men twenty minutes to pull him inch by inch from the treacherous mire.

This interruption over, the party crawled on, stopping constantly to pick up the lost trail. Falls were frequent, holes abounded, and débris was everywhere. Every few seconds Verey lights rushed into the sky, and the men stood stock still until the glare faded. Showers of bullets usually followed, and shells burst intermittently.

For some hours fortune smiled on them, and the enemy did not appear to have observed them, but suddenly a storm of shells burst in their midst, and hell broke loose. They staggered on doggedly for a few minutes, hoping that there would be a respite, but none came and the men sank down on the sodden earth, heaving and shaking with the terrific explosions, and waited wearily.

Dawn was breaking as they fell into " Jolting Horse " Trench, and throughout the day they lay exhausted in any cover they could find, except when they were detailed for fatigues that took them out into the downpour of rain, and heavier particles. Reaction set in rapidly and Lambert, ill and sick, crawled under a large baulk of timber like a beaten dog, and lay like dead for hours, entirely oblivious of the world outside.

The scene at " The Mound " the next night is too ghastly for description. Thousands of wounded had been brought to the Aid Post, until the dug-outs were filled to overflowing, and perforce the poor fellows had to lay outside. The Germans had "strafed" it unmercifully, killing doctors, and many men, and converting the whole area into a shambles.

How Lambert got along the duck-board track to Hooge Crater he never knew. Nature had mercifully thrown a veil over feeling, and his limbs worked mechanically. Throughout the night he toiled on, staggering from side to side like a man in the last stages of intoxication. Dozens of times he tripped over boards, fell with a crash and lay prone for several minutes. Now and again he stepped off the boards into the mud, which sucked at him greedily, and only instinct inspired the effort necessary to extricate himself.

Eleven hours after leaving " Jolting Horse" Trench, he was assisted out of a limber at Zillebeke Lake. He was plastered with mud from head to foot; his face was yellow and lined like an old man's, five days' growth of stubble was on his chin; his rifle was unrecognisable, and was covered from muzzle to butt with a layer of evil-smelling mud, while his puttees had fallen with the weight and clung round his boots like great bowls.

Beach Thomas summed up his dreadful appearance when he said: "The men coming out of the trenches at Ypres were like men risen from the dead!"

A certain number of the battalion had been kept behind, and had waited all night for the survivors who dribbled in. Lambert fell into the arms of his oldest friend, the tenor singer, who helped him along to some mud bivouacs, brought him hot tea, and only recognised him by his voice.

The drink revived him to some extent, and sitting on a mud bank he gazed wearily around. Little knots of men were dotted here and there, talking spasmodically, their faces working with emotion. A tall company commander was striding up and down, hands behind his back and chin down on his breast. Somebody saw Lambert and hurried up to him.

"Where's Roberts, Brown, Carter?" he asked.

"I dunno," murmured Lambert dully.

The questioner subsided on to the bank, and burst into a flood of tears.

Several men led Lambert to a cavern, and *peeled* him of boots, puttees and socks, but he was asleep before they had finished.

CHAPTER IX

"REWARDS" AT METEREN

It seemed cruel to move the shattered battalion a few hours later, but so dreadful and continuous was the fighting for Passchendaele Ridge, that no sooner had one brigade done its awful part than another had to be flung into the furnace, and "advanced billets" were scarce.

A pitiful handful limped through Dickebusch. A mixture of the fortunate fellows who had not been in the attack, and the human wrecks who had. All were drawn and haggard, but sprinkled here and there were men whose frightful appearance advertised their recent experiences.

They rested at the first green space outside the salient, and the place seemed to be haunted by the ghosts of those who were not there. Each muddy unshaven man had a circle of mournful questioners, and Lambert realised, after a few seconds, the impossibility of explaining more than an infinitesimal portion of the operations, or the fate of men concerned in other portions of the attack. All his particular friends had gone and he felt isolated and lonely.

As they lay on the damp clay, a party of the Warwicks passed along the road. It was headed by the band, but no instruments were being played. A few men followed, scarcely more than twenty, and the H.A.C. waited for the rest of the battalion, which belonged to their Brigade. There was no "rest." It had gone to swell the cost of winning Passchendaele Ridge.

"REWARDS" AT METEREN

It is a long walk from Zillebeke to Meteren, but the H.A.C. had to do it, and the next day at dusk saw them climbing a hill from compact, ill-fated little Bailleul, and filing into dark noisome barns.

Memories had to be drowned somehow during those overcast days of October, and they were drowned fairly successfully. Meteren had known British troops since 1914, when the Germans had been driven out at the point of the bayonet, and rumour had it that a Highlander and German had fallen together from the towering church steeple, locked in a grip of hate.

There were estaminets in plenty, selling just the beverages that Tommy liked, served by vivacious women who knew that the singing of Army songs, in piquant broken English would always meet with applause. Almost every house supplied succulent dishes of eggs, cooked in every conceivable manner, and there was an assortment of confectionery and sweetmeats to delight the heart that had sickened of bully or stew.

Passes were granted for Bailleul, only two kilos down the hill, where there were restaurants and shops, and even the "pictures" which, with unique discernment, were "featuring" the "Battle of Arras," possibly as a reminder to the resting troops that war still existed.

Most of them tried to forget it for a few days, but the Army devotees had ideas of their own regarding "rests." Orders tumbled over one another's heels. Every trace of mud must disappear—leather must gleam—buckles must shine in the sun (if any), hair must be cut—not a minute particle of dust must be visible on or in the rifle—manual drill must be practised. Every conceivable kind of "posh" must happen, and some battalion commanders would have ordered their men's memories to be thoroughly scoured if it had been possible.

Lambert groaned as he heard the unending list.

Continuous inhaling of cordite fumes, exposure, and mental and physical torture had completely upset his system and he could only lie inert on his small portion of straw. He had gone sick, been given a "No. 9," which had brought no relief, but had produced waves of sickness that recurred spasmodically throughout the day and night.

Feebly as a child he scraped the thick covering of mud from everything he possessed and duly visited the barber, as sharply ordered by the new sergeant-major, his old platoon sergeant. Ordered to parade early next morning, he fought down the desire to "go sick" once more and slouched out into the cobbled yard that served for parade ground.

The officer walked along the ranks, inspecting the clipped locks.

"Why aren't your buttons cleaned ? " he demanded sharply. Lambert did not answer.

"Put this man down for a fatigue, sergeant-major."

"Man's puttees are dirty, sir ! " was that gentleman's contribution.

"Give him a double fatigue ! "

Sweeping roads is not calculated to improve the mind and it is certainly no cure for a disordered stomach, but Lambert shouldered a broom next morning and spent his thirty-fourth birthday removing mud, etcetera, from the streets of Meteren. The result was not encouraging for his ailment, and when he returned to the barn his gloom was not lightened by the news that the commanding officer would inspect rifles the next morning, and that his comrades had spent the day removing the collection of Ypres slime.

The barn was illumined by a few candles, but Lambert fought down the sickness that made him long for sleep, and in the dim light scraped, rubbed and oiled the clay stick that was really a rifle. In

"REWARDS" AT METEREN

his misery he did not remember the teeth of the backsight (of which there are over forty in the four inch "leaf"), and when he dropped back upon his pallet, the rifle looked clean and bright, but there was a tiny quota of mud in each of those little teeth.

There were a lot of temporary promotions among the officers the next morning and the senior-exercised his wit on all and sundry. He took Lambert's rifle, and twisted it with the dexterity of long practice, while the Acting Adjutant, Acting Company Commander, Acting Platoon Officer, Regimental-Sergeant-Major, Acting Company-Sergeant-Major and the Acting Platoon Sergeant waited for the *bon-mot*. The inspecting officer started to return the rifle, and then drew it back and his eyes fixed themselves on the teeth of the backsight.

"Ha!" he said triumphantly. "You could grow vegetables in here!"

The rifle was handed back and somebody made a note in a book, and later on Lambert was informed that he was to appear at the Battalion Orderly Room the next morning.

He was acquainted with the mud of Meteren, so that it was no new experience to stand in the gutter outside a small house that served for headquarters, although the squirts of mud that shot at him from passing motors were rather disconcerting. He was not the only offender that morning, and to his great surprise, the man who had helped his company commander back, and the loose-limbed youth who had volunteered to carry down wounded after the recent tragedy, were also lined up in the roadway.

Before he could whisper an inquiry, he was suddenly ordered to quick march, his cap was knocked off, and he halted before a retinue of officers.

"Good man in the line, but slack out of it," said his acting company commander.

Filled with disgust, Lambert did not attempt

to bring forward any such circumstances as exhaustion, or moral and physical disability, but simply mentioned that the rifle had been cleaned in a dark billet. A cutting comment, the forfeiture of five days' pay as a punishment, and he was marched out to the doorstep, where his cap awaited him.

He lingered in the vicinity, anxious to congratulate his two friends upon the rewards for their bravery. Both acts had roused in him a strong sense of admiration, and his own experience was nearly forgotten. A long interval elapsed before they appeared, and the looks on their faces did not in the least suggest satisfaction or pleasure. An eager inquiry produced the astonishing statement from both, that they had been charged with the loss of their equipments, and fined the regulation price for the same.

In the one case the defence that one could not carry a heavy stretcher over narrow duck-boards, laden with rifle and equipment, had been dismissed abruptly, and in the other, an almost unanswerable plea of acting under instructions, had met the astonishing reply that the "wounded officer had not been in a fit condition to give orders!"

A gloomy trio wandered back to billets, filled to the brim with horror and disgust. Instead of recommendations for bravery, or appreciation of endurance in appalling conditions, they had been "run" for trifles, and punishments had been inflicted that disgraced the judges, and not the prisoners.

Hatred of a system that could allow such injustice filled Lambert's soul that night. The "rewards" for the living; the forgotten heroism of the dead; the instantaneous return to ancient, obsolete barrack-square methods; the horrible ignorance of the fact that the "civilian" army was brain and nerve, as well as bone and muscle, appalled his logical mind, and the thought that practically every chum in his platoon had suffered in an endeavour to add glory

"REWARDS" AT METEREN

to this system brought a lump into his throat. He gulped it down as a flashlamp sent its white ray across the barn, and a loud voice inquired for a man in the platoon who had "gone over the top" at Passchendaele.

Instinctively Lambert answered civilly.

"Are you a man of average intelligence?"

"Occasionally," returned Lambert drily.

The Acting Adjutant made his way across the crowded forms of sleepy men, and fired off a stream of questions, which were answered without hesitation. The scene was photographed on Lambert's brain, and he was able to describe it graphically and to foil attempts to prove that left was right and vice versa.

Recent events had affected his view concerning officers very considerably, and he withstood his ground steadily during a fierce cross-examination which endeavoured to move a cemetery from one side of a field to another. Sharp retorts, and a sketch map from him settled the point.

The questions became more personal and Lambert described at length the orders given and the steps taken by his platoon sergeant, now Acting Sergeant-Major. Pride in his platoon lent him enthusiasm, and every detail that might rebound to the man's credit was diluted upon at some length, and not a little eloquence. The Adjutant appeared almost satisfied and retired. Next morning some instinct moved Lambert to recount the conversation to his new Sergeant Major.

"You'll get the D.C.M., sir!" he ended finally, with an air of conviction.

"*Some* ruddy hope," was the answer.

When the battalion marched back along the road to Ypres, after ten days at Meteren, the companies were two platoon strong, and Lambert found himself among many new acquaintances. They did not hesitate to comment upon his recent adventures, and dubbed him the "man who got the C.S.M. the D.C.M."

Human nature demonstrates itself in many strange forms. From that day the Company-Sergeant-Major lost no opportunity of exercising a caustic wit, and bestowing plenty of fatigues, upon the private.

CHAPTER X

THE STRETCHER-BEARING "STUNT"

"FATIGUE," in the Army rendering of the word, embraces any and every job that men can attempt. All forms of energy, from fetching food to erecting barbed wire in "No-Man's Land," are "fatigues," and the infantry were utilised for any unit that required help.

It is upon record that a distinguished visitor to the front stopped to watch a crowd of men hauling timber, and inquired if they were a Labour Battalion.

"Oh! no, sir," was the reply. "They are infantry resting!"

The H.A.C. had earned a reputation for good work in and out of the line, and there were few units that had not had the use of their services. The R.A.M.C. wanted help now. Fighting during those days in October did not cease, and the whole area was littered with the dreadful results. Help was desperately needed by the over-worked "medicos," and one hundred men from the H.A.C. were detailed to carry down wounded.

They started in the early hours one morning, carrying their food with them, and marched the long road to the "advanced aid posts" just behind those dreadful front lines. The enemy shelled them all the way up, shelled them while they waited for their burdens of pain, and shelled them as they carried the wounded back.

The weather had been persistently wet and the district was a sea of mud, which lapped over the duck-boards as the men slid over them with the stretchers. For forty-eight hours those brave fellows struggled along the narrow tracks until their physical exhaustion was pitiful. Despite all their efforts, slips and falls were inevitable on the muddy boards, and the mental agony of letting a badly-wounded man down cannot be described. The hungry mud tried to snatch victims time after time. Stretchers would tip as one of the bearers slipped, and the occupants would slip immediately into the treacherous slime, unless extricated by main force.

Shells burst everywhere, killing wounded and stretcher-bearers indiscriminately, or adding to the wounds of poor fellows already groaning with pain.

Together with manual drill, Army recruits learned Army language, which is forcible and usually redundant. Some men knew the language before they joined up, others took to it very quickly and used it on every possible (and impossible) occasion, but here and there were men who adhered steadfastly to civilian expressions.

One of these was helping to carry a stretcher along those dreadful tracks. He was weak with physical effort, lack of food and mental strain. The wounded men were heavy, and it was raining hard with hot metal and cold water. Suddenly he slipped off the duck-board into a particularly spongy shell hole, and the hungry mud enveloped him to the neck with a horrible sucking noise. Fortunately he shot out his hands in time, and his fingers gripped the edge of the wood.

If ever strong language was justified this was the moment, but the man immortalised himself by exclaiming mildly, " Oh, blow ! "

Terrible as the work was in daylight, it was indescribable at night when the only light was that of bursting shells. Just before actual darkness set in, a German aeroplane, flying very low, raced over and raked the

STRETCHER-BEARING "STUNT"

line of men with its machine gun. Probably this was called "harassing the enemy." Whatever its description, the act was one of those innumerable incidents in the "Great War," that was an offence to God and man.

Throughout those long hours of physical agony, the men struggled along without food. They had brought plenty, but one cannot carry a heavy stretcher and a bag of rations at the same time, and so continuous was the work that few had an opportunity of trying to obtain sustenance. They simply staggered on until their work became an epic of endurance and heroism.

"The party" had marched out of billets on Thursday morning, and a percentage of them reeled back in the early hours of Saturday, exhausted, famished and aching in every muscle of the body, after the most sustained and distressing form of energy conceivable. It will be many years before the survivors of that "fatigue" will forget the stretcher-bearing "stunt" at Ypres.

CHAPTER XI

GHELUVELT

" BEGGARS' REST FARM," on the swampy road leading to "Swan and Edgar," was not prettily named, although the artistic might prefer the title to "Dead Dog Farm," which adjoined it, but the name was certainly the best part of it. Muddy tents, with dripping canvas and oozing floors, stood in waterlogged fields into which the feet sank at every step, and the whole presented a picture of utter misery.

Opposite the entrance, on a narrow strip of grassland, Lambert and three others sat in pools of water beneath a leaking tarpaulin. They were bounded on three sides by high stacks of bombs and ammunition, which they had been wearily collecting from Brandenburg Dump, and stacking throughout a long wet day.

Now they awaited the regiment marching from Dickebusch to take possession of "advanced rest billets." Nobody knew what was in store for them, but they were within a mile of that fearsome Menin Road and all the horror beyond it, and as the dusk deepened the country shook with the roar of our guns, and the incessant bombing of German aircraft.

The corporal in charge sat stolidly in his damp seat, sucking continuously at his pipe. He was a cheery, even-tempered individual, with a most powerful Cambridge accent, who was known to all as "Lottie," and his chief vice was the incessant smoking of the strongest shag. Fumes from his pipe nearly asphyxiated Lambert. They made him cough and splutter, brought tears to his eyes and gasping curses up his throat.

GHELUVELT

"What infernal muck are you smoking, Lottie?" he asked savagely.

"Aw! Dam' good baccy, Lambo," drawled the corporal. "'Faulkner's Nosegay.' Have a fill, what?"

Lambert declined emphatically, and impatiently endured the torment, hating "Faulkner's Nosegay" more thoroughly every minute, until the tramping of feet made a move necessary, and proclaimed the fact that the remnants of the battalion had arrived at their watery lodgings.

It was the 25th of October, and in a mysterious way the news ran round the camp that another great attack was to be made at daybreak the next morning by one of the brigades in their division—the 91st. Wet at all times, the district now was almost impassable, the pitiless rain had not ceased for hours, and there was no break in the leaden sky. Hour after hour went by and still the downpour continued, and when night fell there was no cessation.

Conversation languished and faces lengthened as the dark hours slowly passed. Bad weather seemed to dog the footsteps of the British Army, and in no place was rain more unwelcome than in the Ypres salient. Hearts ached for the unfortunates waiting in the mud-holes for the "Zero" hour; gloomy thoughts kept swinging back to the fact that the Jocks, Queens and Manchesters would have to face a worse enemy than the inevitable storm of shot or shell, the clinging mud of the stricken land.

Many prayers were whispered that the rain would cease, or the attack be "washed out," but they were not answered. Just before dawn the tents shook with the shattering vibrations of our artillery barrage.

It had rained for over twenty-four hours when a sudden order came from Brigade, and the remainder of the battalion paraded for an immediate move. They were laden to the eyes with Lewis guns, ammunition, bombs, and signalling paraphernalia, and the hurried alarm smacked ominously of reinforcements for the front line.

"Easy job this time," said the Sergeant-Major, and it was many hours later before the party concluded that the remark was a specimen of sardonic humour.

All through the afternoon the men trudged along the timber road, bestrewn with the terrible evidences of war. Their loads were appallingly heavy, each step reproduced a gasp of exertion and quite a number of the older men wept with exhaustion. Lambert was so heavy that he could hardly lift one foot from the other, and had to be pulled by men with lighter burdens up sudden rises in the track. It was impossible to walk many yards without falling, and each time the effort to get up was almost incredible. On one of these occasions Lambert heard a sharp crack and groaned mournfully. Another pipe smashed!

In the evening the men rested on the side of a steep, muddy ridge, and vicious prolonged curses broke out as the leaden minutes dragged on. The British Army does not wear overcoats; it only carries them. Everybody was very cold in that chilly, sopping atmosphere; they had been rushed up, only to wait hours on this mud bank, and there were the crashes of shells every second exceedingly near them.

Lambert found himself next to the officer who had "run him," and an overwhelming desire to be impudent mastered him.

"Can we smoke, sir?" he asked blandly.

The officer reflected for a moment, and his answer completely disarmed the private.

"I don't think we had better. Those shells are quite near enough, aren't they?"

The private lay quiet, sucking sweets that had arrived from that lovely land so many millions of miles away, idly speculating as to the next spot to be hit by a shell, and wondering if that artillery officer,

GHELUVELT

observing so quietly a hundred yards away, had cold feet.

Pattering feet sounded from the top of the ridge, and down the duck-board track came a few Gordon Highlanders. They were plastered from head to foot and raced along like stags. Their eyes were glued on the track, and they paid not the slightest attention to the waiting men. Short gasps escaped them as they leapt clumsily over the shattered body of an R.A.M.C. lying across the path. There were about twenty of them, and survivors of a glorious battalion.

In that downpour of rain they had advanced to the attack. Forcing their way through a morass that enveloped them to their waists, they had ploughed slowly towards their objective in a frenzy of gigantic strength and undying courage. Shells of all kinds had crashed into them; swathes of machine gun bullets had found human billets, but the remainder ploughed on and had taken their position, although every man's rifle was clogged with mud, and unworkable.

Battalions on their left and right had advanced with the utmost gallantry, but lacking the superhuman strength of the Jocks had failed to fulfil their allotted tasks. The Gordons had held on like heroes, although enfiladed on each side, but it was certain death to remain, and they retired across the lake of mud, followed by the pitiless hail of bullets. They lost heavily in the advance, but were practically wiped out in the retreat, and the other battalions were in the same dreadful condition.

Subsequent descriptions of the sustained battle for Passchendaele Ridge contain such phrases as " terribly costly " ; " failure " ; " unparalleled casualties," and so on. No adjectives can describe the carnage. Every battalion that attacked that sombre spot came out a grisly shadow, and it was sheer murder to attack under such dreadful conditions.

Over this stricken field the H.A.C. crept in the darkness, seeking the elusive shell holes occupied by the actors in the recent tragedy. Delays were frequent, and brave boys swelled the awful total of casualties, hit by the bullets that swished incessantly. At last the jagged line was found and the poor remnants of the 91st Brigade disappeared into the darkness while the H.A.C. dug like fiends in soupy bottoms of shell-holes, until daylight made the work dangerous.

There are few stranger scenes than a battlefield " the day after." An expanse of mud, dotted with the dark spots of shell holes ; a dreary pitiless nothingness, except for a few trunks of shattered trees, a heap of bricks, or barbed wire pickets lolling drunkenly here and there. No sound except the occasional whine of a long-distance shell, or the sharp crack of a sniper's rifle. No sign of human beings except those forms lying so still in the mud that they seemed part of it, or quivering gently at times as though stirred by the breeze.

Lambert sickened at the number of them, as he stared into the trench periscope fixed to his bayonet. He had seen similar sights seventeen days before, on that portion of the ridge a mile or two to the left, and it was horrifying to think of the many bloody battles during that period, and the uncountable times over the same ground during three long years.

Slowly he twisted the periscope round, visualising the scanty landmarks. Almost callously he noticed the positions of the dead and unrecovered wounded, but he was glad when a sniper's bullet shivered the mirror into fragments. Just above the lip of the shell hole there was the figure of a young man, crouching as if to spring, both sets of finger-tips resting on the ground, one leg stretched behind him, the other drawn up under his body. The tin hat, gas mask and equipment were still on, and there was no sign of injury, but " it " crouched there like the most perfect representation of the sculptor's art.

The six men composing his section huddled on a shelf

that they had cut in the wet shell hole; another half a dozen were twenty yards off, and there were other parties dotted about in an irregular line. All tried to keep their feet dry, but there was no foothold on the slippery sides, and tired Nature asserted itself time after time, and the freezing water crept into their boots.

There was nothing to do except to watch in turns. Both sides were resting after an exhausting fight; reserves were coming up and the lines were being stealthily repaired. Only the snipers kept busy and they fired at the slightest target. In those gloomy and tragic surroundings Lambert supplied a comic note. His feet were in six inches of water, his face was muddy, and streaked with oily dirt from the bombs he had carried. He was wearing a drab ground-sheet, and a woollen cap comforter tied in a huge bow round his neck, while he sucked at a pipe bowl with only half an inch of stem. It was a relief to look at him and laugh.

Tragedy followed hard upon Comedy's heel. The bulky figure of a company "runner" appeared on the edge of the hole, and dropped in precipitately. In gasps he told them that the officer had sent him for a sergeant from one of the advanced shell holes, and the snipers had tried to get him several times on the way back.

"Bit hot sending in the daylight," he panted. "Sergeant didn't care about it either. Wouldn't come back with me. Didn't like moving a bit. Those swines——"

Several shots rang out in quick succession and another man dropped in amongst them. Wiping his white forehead, the sergeant sorted himself out and looked round the shell hole, his mouth drooping with horror as he finished the survey.

"Mr —— not here?" he gasped. "Not here? Heavens. This game will be the death of me!"

They pointed out the larger hole twenty yards left, and the sergeant mopped his brow again, his eyes wandering round their set faces. Suddenly he crouched, charged to the side of the hole, dashed like a deer across the intervening ground and hesitated on the very edge of safety.

"Get in!" screamed Lambert. "My—God!"

Premonition was only too terribly true. Just about to plunge into comparative safety, a rifle with a fixed bayonet propped against the side of the shell hole barred his path, and during a second's pause, a sniper had ended the poor man's earthly career.

Nobody moved during the rest of that day, but sat and slowly froze. Feet got colder and colder until numbness took away all sense of feeling. Persistent massage kept other parts of the body fairly warm.

At dusk the Germans opened a furious bombardment that made hands grasp rifles in anticipation of an attack. Great shells raced over, bursting with tremendous force in all directions, sending large fragments of case hurtling through the air. One whizzed by Lambert's ear as he stood on the look-out step, and buried itself with a thud between the open knees of a comrade sitting below. It was still hot when they dug it out, and it acted as an excellent "hot potato" for their cold hands.

Machine gun bullets swept round in great circles, and from behind, half a dozen shells burst immediately in front of their post. Lambert jumped down with a splash into the pool. For the first time in many hours he felt a warm glow run through him.

"Our trench-mortars," he gasped. "Short."

They sat through the long night, and in the morning a mantle of frost covered them from head to foot. During the weary hours, a young man from Australia pleaded with Lambert for warmth, and gratefully accepted an invitation to sit on his lap, and be cuddled like a great baby.

There is no need to describe at length the following day. Words cannot adequately portray the painful

GHELUVELT

crawl of the hours, the slow transition from acute agony to semi-unconscious painlessness, the dull apathy of the mind and nerves, varied by the throbbing heart, or the fierce rush of the chilled blood, shocked into sudden activity.

Long-awaited relief came in the force of business-like Cheshires, who descended upon them in a swarm, while after a few hurried details as to the position the H.A.C. disappeared just as hurriedly into the darkness.

It was the work of a few minutes and seldom was relief effected more expeditiously. A race to "get out" ensued, and down the duck-boards hurried the panting soldiers, stopping only when Verey lights shot into the dark sky, silhouetting them in their brilliance, and producing the inevitable scream of machine gun fire.

One platoon was ordered to wait while the officer visited Brigade Headquarters, but it was "Get to 'Shrapnel Corner, and every man for himself !" with the rest, and Lambert marvelled at their speed. He kept up with them for half a mile, until the exercise brought his feet back to life, and then speed was out of the question. Ten thousand red-hot needles pierced the flesh at every step, causing exquisite pain and making speed impossible. Limbs and head were aching and over him crept the familiar nausea that cordite invariably produced.

He dropped behind, losing ground at every step, reeling and staggering along mechanically, head drooping and knees sagging. Out of some unintelligible dream, a voice stirred his drooping faculties.

"H.A.C. ?" it asked.

"Lam-Lambert, A. Company," he mumbled.

An exclamation of delight was the reply, and Lambert dimly recognised his tenor friend who had met him after the attack nearly three weeks ago. Practical sympathy was forthcoming in the shape of a brandy flask, and arm in arm the two men slowly progressed along the interminable road to "Shrapnel Corner."

Lights danced before Lambert's eyes; his feet throbbed as though each contained a dynamo, and his lips were so parched that a cigarette hung pendulously from the skin.

Hours seemed to pass, but the singer helped the exhausted man along with infinite patience, encouraging him by words, taking his weight time after time without remonstrance, and slowly but surely guiding him to that ill-famed corner, where lorries waited to take them out of that awful district.

In the lorry the world went round Lambert as he squatted on the mass of equipment, with his arm round his friend's neck. Deadly faintness attacked him, but he fought instinctively and eventually conquered the weakness. He woke to hear a medley of noises. A popular song, bawled at the top of men's voices, the drone of approaching aeroplanes, followed quickly by a series of appalling crashes.

" Jerry " dropped bombs all round those lorries, but the singing increased in volume. Damn bombs! Damn the Germans! They were going " OUT ! "

A long delay, waiting in vain for the officer and his platoon who had lingered at B.H.Q., and the lorries took them " out." Out of the land of terrible death, hideous wounds and indescribable putrescence into green fields, pure air, and relief from trials too heavy for flesh and blood to bear.

The missing officer and his platoon arrived eight hours later. They had come some miles from Brigade Headquarters in gas masks while the enemy plastered the sector with three thousand gas shells.

Half an hour later the survivors of one attack on Passchendaele Ridge were marching on the cobbly road that led away from the salient!

" They say we shall not go back to Ypres," somebody said to Lambert.

" I hope to God we never do," he returned, and never uttered a more fervent prayer.

CHAPTER XII

FAREWELL TO FLANDERS

EARLY one morning in November, the depleted Seventh Division stamped the sodden grass of a field into mud, blew on its fingers, and used other time-honoured methods for keeping warm. They had stood there for over an hour, and the air was damp and chilly. In compact masses, battalions were paraded on the side of a long slope, for one of those unknown functions that occur so frequently in a soldier's life.

Sturdy Highlanders, stocky Manchesters and Staffords, assorted Queen's and H.A.C.'s met in slightly different conditions than in recent weeks, and there were many shouted inquiries from one unit to the other. All agreed as to the unprintable adjectives describing the Ypres battles.

A sudden word of command, and talking ceased instantly, and the multitude of figures stiffened. Massed bands commenced the first notes of "La Brabançonne," as a small cavalcade galloped on the field. A long-drawn-out order from the General; a smacking of rifles, and the whole division came to the "present," and stood erect and stiff.

A tall, fair, grim-looking man on a magnificent black charger rode slowly along the ranks. There was no sign of emotion visible; no pride or sorrow, only a cold hauteur on features that seemed to be carved in wax. And yet every man who saw Albert of Belgium ride past, so erect and steady in his seat that he seemed to form part of that fine horse, felt that here was a proper king.

The man cantered along the mass of men who had fought for that strip of sodden bog that remained of Belgium, then stood at the saluting-post like a gigantic statue, with a background of officers dressed in every kind of uniform.

Another sharp order, and every cap twirled in the air three times, while the owners shouted cheers in obedience to orders.

Further commands, and like well-oiled machines, battalions swung round, marched up the slope, wheeled, and came down the hill at a swinging pace; a splendid phalanx of bayonets that gleamed in the leaden atmosphere of that November day.

As they approached the saluting-post, every head turned towards the kingly statue, whose hand was raised to the salute as though attached by invisible clasps.

A hurried rush across ploughed fields to prevent congestion, and the review was over.

"That's good-bye to Belgium!" said a well-informed person as they trudged back to their odorous billets.

It was quite true. The tragedy or scandal (which you will) of Caporetto was convulsing Europe. Our Italian allies were retreating from the Tagliamento and nobody knew where they would stop. The Allied Council had met at Versailles, decided to send English and French divisions to Italy, and after receiving reinforcements, the 7th Division packed its thousands of sundries and tramped wearily to the railway station.

BOOK TWO
ITALY

CHAPTER I

"IN THE TRAIN"

Few people in England have wondered how armies move; fewer still have seen the process in operation; but on the Continent, long dirty trucks, inscribed, *Hommes* 40, *Chevaux* 8, were common sights.

Lambert had travelled with thirty-nine companions on one occasion, and was just about to die of asphyxiation when the journey ended. Hauling himself in a truck with a grunt of exertion, he devoutly hoped that there would be no attempt to realise the maximum number this time.

Thirty men crowded in, and for half an hour it seemed impossible to accommodate them and their mountain of equipment, but the soldier is an adaptable animal. Out of strange pockets came nails, the entrenching tool handle was an admirable hammer, and in a short space of time there was a furious outburst of nailing. Very soon equipments, rifles, tin hats, gas masks and articles *ad infinitum* were hanging on pegs, candles were glimmering, and men were sitting on their packs, getting cool after the heavy march.

They were quite self-supporting. In the tremendously long train there were men and horses, food and cooking appliances, limbers, wagons, water carts, stores of wood, leather, clothing and sundries too numerous to mention.

There were huge quantities of ammunition. Every brigade carried its own reserve of small man-killing

material, which they " dumped " in a given place.
When the Brigade moved the dump did the same,
and there was always the anomaly of moving say,
100,000 cartridges, and the relieving brigade
" dumping " the same quantity in the same spot.

Hours passed before the long train started with a
jerk that severely tested insecure nails, and brought
their burdens down with a crash on the man below,
sometimes the careless owner and sometimes not.
There was no cheering or enthusiasm from civilians ;
a fine regimental band played the train out, and a
few fortunates staying behind at the Base waved hats,
but, apart from this, the troop train started on its long
journey quietly.

Emotions were very mixed. It was a relief to
leave the Western front, with its eternal mud and
cracking shells, but the Colonel warned them that they
might have to get out of the train and fight, and
alternately they were to accept any rapturous welcome
from the Italian people with becoming modesty,
but were not to accept wine.

They were going to a strange country, and the future
was very uncertain. Italy was so far away from England
and the possibility of getting back so remote. In
France and Belgium the chances of getting a " Blighty "
were always speculated upon, and already news had
filtered through of comrades who had received
" cushy " ones at Passchendaele reaching the land of all
their hopes. There was no chance of " getting one "
in Italy, land anding home within twenty-four hours.

Lambert felt very down-hearted. All his friends
had gone ; he was alone in a new crowd of reinforcements from the first battalion, and each mile was
taking him farther away from his villa with its clematis
and roses, his splendid boys and loving wife ! In
addition, letters had been delayed, pay-days scarce,
and he was starting a terrific journey with seven
francs.

It was a miserable prospect, but the cloud lifted as each hour bumped them farther away. To his delight he recognised Bright among the forms squatting at the other end of the truck. He had left him at Havre two months before, but it was like a searchlight in the gloom to see a friendly face. Forces were promptly joined, another five francs added to the joint stock, and the two friends compared notes well into the night.

That first night! The heavy doors were crashed to, and the thirty men tried to lay full length—feet to head. It was almost impossible, and legs were curled up in all kinds of cramping positions. A sergeant dropping into a heavy sleep crooked his knees, and crushed Lambert's legs against the sides of the truck until he freed them with a desperate effort. Ventilation there was none; the air became soupy and heavy; facilities for natural functions were non-existent, and men afflicted with a complaint always prevalent in the Army suffered agonies. Just at the moment when everybody was in a troubled sleep, the train would jolt violently, and throughout the night the springless truck bumped violently over the poor track.

Halting points were on the time-table, where the troops could clean themselves and have some hot meals, but the last thing a troop train does is to keep time, and frequently the halts occurred in the middle of the night. To wait many hours for a cup of tea, get down without it, and be aroused at three o'clock on a chilly morning, was a fine lesson in self-control.

There were dozens of stops every day, but the men soon became accustomed to the new conditions, and made merry in the inimitable military manner. They sang all the songs in their extensive repertoire, joked and read, waved hands at any female, of any age, and purchased any possible article of food that came their way.

They were forbidden to leave the train, but enterprising French " garçons," or " filles," ran like deers on hundreds of errands, and were responsible for many minor tragedies. Lambert and Bright groaned with horror when a boy delivered an appetising loaf, which they paid for, to the wrong man three trucks away, just as the train started. They were on bully and granite biscuits, and the loaf had cost one of their last francs !

The trail of the British Army was " blazed " in an unmistakable manner from Northern France, round the outskirts of Paris, through the Midland provinces, and down the lovely valley of the Rhône. Along these hundreds of miles of line there was an unending " spoor " of thousands of empty bully beef tins.

Several days after the mirk and mire of Belgium had gone, the train ran into Fairyland. Lovely verdant hills stretched away on one side, dotted with beautifully tinted villas nestling in the palms and orange groves. Roses in full bloom climbed their walls, and rare plants blossomed in the open. On the other side, wooded shaded walks skirted the blue sea, whose sunny waves lapped gently against the golden sands.

Through Cannes, Nice, Mentone and Monte Carlo, " Tommy Atkins " gazed entranced. It was heaven after the horror of Ypres and Gheluvelt, and the men, many deep at the doors, watched the moving panorama with astonished eyes, and inhaled the warm breezes of the incomparable Riviera with unalloyed delight.

At several of these towns warm-hearted ladies of different nationalities dispensed gifts of tobacco, cigarettes and good wishes. Bright smiles from charming faces met them everywhere, and it was well into that particular night before the Italian Expeditionary Force retired to " bed." Lambert was handed a gift by a charming woman and found, on examination, that it was an ounce of Faulkner's Nosegay.

IN THE TRAIN

They awoke in Italy, and spirits dropped with a thud that was almost audible. A grey mist hung over a flat plain covered with fields of maize stalks, lolling black and sodden in all directions. There were few houses in sight, and little sign of life, but over everything brooded a drab fog that neutralised any bright colours that might have existed. The plains of Lombardy are always referred to as rich and fertilised, and wars have been fought for them, but on that November day they did not look worth a bullet.

A few Italian soldiers lolled about the larger stations, and the first impression was not favourable. They were mostly unshaven and shabby; critical eyes noted dirty boots, dull leather and rusty bayonets, and in return the dark faces displayed little interest and less friendliness. Caporetto was very recent and the memory hurt!

The train clanked on for interminable hours, but there was no sign of war. Practice in loading cartridges had been a feature of the journey, with muzzles carefully pointed at the landscape, but there was no rumble of artillery in the distance, shell-pocked fields, or ruined homes.

Scarcely any of the men knew where they were, fewer still their ultimate destination, but it was all-sufficient knowledge, when they de-trained after a week of life in a truck, that it was not to fight immediately, and cheers! it was rumoured that the staff were fixing billets for the night.

There were hours to wait (there always were in the Army from enlistment to discharge) and the night was cold, but the H.A.C. started fires, and sat round in huge circles singing glees and hymns. Sung them beautifully, and many a man choked down a lump as the volumes of sound rose into the clear Italian sky.

Eventually they marched into a village, where

white buildings stood out tall and ghostly in the bright moonlight. The hour was late and not a light or person was visible. The place seemed completely deserted, not even a cat or dog came out to stare at the "Inglese," and as the companies filed into schools and municipal buildings, Lambert and Bright argued fiercely as to whether the town was within the war zone and completely evacuated or not.

Lambert felt that his trousers were unusually damp, and found that he had been sitting for an hour or two in a pool of petrol, which left a mark on the garments that many months' wear did not eradicate.

CHAPTER II

A WALK ACROSS ITALY

How the sun shines in Italy! It was a revelation to the English, accustomed to months of leaden sky, weeks of rain and a few faint gleams of sunshine for hours every day.

Everything was frozen stiff when the men awoke for their first day, but the warm radiance delighted them, and little parties soon scoured every street and shop in the village. There was a tremendous run on the bakery, where a poor, shrivelled old woman dispensed hot loaves in a bewildered, scared manner, and seemed surprised when the men paid for them.

Soldier-shopping was a very simple affair. Men saw a shop and went into it. They could not speak the language but that was of little consequence. There was nothing in the stock that they wanted, but it was interesting to rummage about, and amusing if they walked out without purchasing anything.

When something was required, strange acting ensued, and if energetic combing of the hair with the fingers resulted in a pot of pomade being produced, it mattered not. Perhaps the next place would pro uce comb.

Men searched the place thoroughly. They soon discovered that many a shop was placed at the end of a dark passage, and that the most attractive emporiums existed behind blank exter ors. The Italian villager did not understand window-dressing and "Tommy" soon found that necessaries were

exceedingly limited, and luxuries were *niente*
(none). He grew to hate *niente* like poison.

Italians looked at the Englishmen with curiosity
and a little envy, and the compliment was returned,
very much minus envy and a great deal of suppressed
mirth. Nobody seemed to live more simply, or poorly,
than these country people, and the masculine costume
of a dark cloak thrown over the shoulders, and a black
sombrero with a feather rampant amused the British
immensely. The women, with their olive skins and
lovely complexions, and invariable kerchief over their
heads, were picturesque, and commanded more
respect.

Evidently the invading Austrians had been held
somewhere, for the reappeared to be no hurry, and the
battalion, instead of being entrained again and rushed
to a military base, commenced a tremendous trek
across Northern Italy. Day after day the men
marched for long hours, covering between thirty and
forty kilos, until at the end of a week there was over
a hundred miles to their credit.

It was a long journey for tired feet and aching
backs, but few fell out. The country was new, and
the horror of marching dwindles when there is a
constant change of scene. Everything interested the
troops. The wonderful banked roads, which were
ascribed to Napoleon, could not have been beaten
for marching; the sun shone brilliantly practically
all day in a sky of lovely blue; the carts and ploughs
drawn by oxen were objects of interest, and fresh
features in the fauna and flora were constantly rising
to distract their attention from the monotony of
marching.

The country was delightfully coloured after drab
Belgium and Northern France. Earth was a rich red;
the vines, although bare of leaf and fruit, were picturesque, trailing from tree to tree or clinging to
carved balconies; large fields of maize gleamed in

A WALK ACROSS ITALY 99

the sun ; and streams of pure crystal ran by the roadside. All the houses were quaint, with their tiled roofs, green shutters and outdoor stairs, and bright pink, green and blue distempers were used with impunity for outside walls. Every house had its painting of a sacred subject or its statue of The Redeemer or the Blessed Virgin, before which were placed lights or pots of flowers.

Many paintings were exceedingly crude, but quite a large proportion presented, at least from a distance, a favourable impression of colour, and here and there were ambitious and artistic designs. Occasionally a house appeared to stand behind a row of silver birches, which were not living, but merely painted on the walls.

The architecture was lovely, and even small farms were impressive with the majesty of the columns supporting the porticos, and the curves of arches leading to the barns. Doorways in ordinary garden walls were works of art, and almost invariably embellished by statues. Every village had its large church, upon which had been lavished all the art at the command of the inhabitants, and each church had its tall " campanile " towering into the blue. From any height there was a vista resembling a gigantic chess board with red, green and yellow squares dotted with innumerable pieces, campanile shaped. Every cemetery was walled and on either side of elaborate wrought iron gates grew tall cypresses standing out black and forbidding against a warm-coloured background.

Shrines were everywhere, and many were illumined at night, even in districts subject to air raids, where all lights were forbidden. Turning a particularly dark corner one night, Lambert and Bright were almost startled by the brilliance of a shrine standing in the centre of a village. It was the statue of the Virgin and Child, perfectly white, illumined by electric light, which stood out against the black background, like a perfect embodiment of purity.

War begets vandalism, as the Germans demonstrated. Passing a large shrine, in a heavy shower of rain, the troops were surprised to see an Italian sentry side by side with a statue of the Virgin, grinning at them from the interior, into which he had climbed to escape getting damp.

The route was almost entirely through rural districts, and no rapturous welcome met them. A few women, old men and children, attracted by the drums and fifes, walked to their gates occasionally, watched stolidly, and returned when the regiment had passed. In the villages people stared at the tramping British, but there was no enthusiasm and certainly no gifts of wine. Printed notices were pasted on walls here and there, with welcome messages such as, " Wiva England," or " Good healt at the Allies."

The latter seemed to suggest an ignorance of idiomatic English, but the British troops were never able to boast of their linguistic abilities. After a year in Italy thousands of men did not get further than " Wine," " to eat," " None," " Bread," " Yes," etc. Lambert knew many men who invariably greeted anybody with *Buona sera* (Good evening) at any time of the morning or night !

A few weeks after the arrival in Italy there were rumours of a serious fight between some Gordon Highlanders and Italians. Apparently some " Jocks " were getting decidedly boisterous in a wine-shop and completely misunderstood the admonition from the Italian proprietor of *Basta !* (enough).

Billets were fresh and clean after the foul barns behind the Western front. Schools, municipal offices, large maize stores and the like were admirable resting places, unless it so happened that one's bed was immediately over the piggery or cattle shed.

On the march one morning, a white wedge-shaped

cloud attracted Lambert's attention. It hung in the sky quite motionless, and kept disappearing at intervals, and then reappearing a different size. The fact was puzzling but interesting to watch, as it diverted attention from inflamed and painful feet. Suddenly the cloud became pink-tipped and stood out boldly in the sunlight.

"Mountains," ejaculated Lambert with a shiver. "Ugh! Don't they look cold!"

The 22nd Infantry Brigade ended their long trek some hours later, and the H.A.C. were billeted in Ramon, a collection of about twenty houses, two shops, ten *vinos*, two hundred chickens and fifty oxen, that nestled on a flat plain overlooked by mighty Monte Grappa.

CHAPTER III

HOME COMFORTS AT RAMON

THOSE delightful people in far-away England who kept the Post Office busy with parcels and letters, could scarcely have appreciated the part they played in the " boys " lives.

Army food, if wholesome, was monotonous, and unpalatable in the extreme. Day after day stew was the principal meal, composed of bully beef or chunks of meat boiled in water. A potato boiled in its jacket, and rice, musty and insipid, without sugar or milk, completed the meal.

Meat suitable for boiling was usually roasted, and vice versa. Whatever the method of cooking it was usually difficult to masticate it. Pastry and fruit were unknown, and a later, indigestible invention called dried vegetables, was used eventually to keep the fires going.

On alternate mornings porridge was served, minus the two ingredients that make it palatable, and about two inches of frightfully salt bacon. Tea was served twice daily, and this was the greatest success of any Army meal. Lambert never touched the porridge or rice, and practically existed on chocolate and dry bread.

It is little wonder that the troops looked anxiously for the parcel mail, with its hope of a few dainties from home, and that they demolished them with the zest of boys at a tuck shop! Letters were even more welcome. The longing for home was intensified by

HOME COMFORTS AT RAMON

the monotony and rigour of the life. Cut off from England, with its food and comfortable beds, books and plays, pictures and music, feminine society, and all the delightful details that go to make up an ordinary life, and dropped into mud and blood, and the appalling monotony of poverty-stricken hamlets, the only solace was to read of the doings, and thoughts, of those beloved ones in " Blighty."

For weeks after leaving France the troops received nothing. Not a parcel arrived to lighten their drooping spirits. They were cut off like the dead, and luxuries were unknown. The canteen remained closed, and the two shops seemed to sell nothing. Lambert and Bright scoured the district for miles round, and considered their energy well rewarded if able to buy a few figs or nuts.

There was an appalling shortage of cigarettes, one of the greatest comforts in the Army. Thousands of men went without smoking for days, or smoked tea leaves wrapped in writing paper. News that a few Italian cigarettes were obtainable in a distant village led to an immediate rush of hundreds of men. Cheap Italian cigarettes need to be smoked for this latter fact to be fully appreciated!

English money could not be changed, and many a man could not buy the cheapest article although his purse was full of notes.

Many of the battalion were billeted in the school and *Municipio*. The rest were scattered about in lofts attached to small farmhouses. These were exposed to the air on two or three sides, and the wind from the snowy Alps nearly cut the men in half. Generally the sun shone brightly during the day, but it became freezingly cold immediately after sunset. All the brooks became icebound, and water bottles lying beside the troops froze solid, and did not melt for weeks.

Entrance and exit from these lofts was by means

of ladders, standing perilously on uneven stones. The beds were composed of maize stalks which were decidedly unfriendly to the human frame desiring rest, and the aroma from the cowhouses below was dense and very highly flavoured.

The maize stalks were many feet deep, and they completely enveloped any small article that was dropped into them. Lambert promptly lost his tooth brush and shaving brush, and failed to buy these articles within a radius of three miles. Evidently Italians did not need these articles. They certainly had good teeth and doubtless, at the end of a week or so, their beards needed professional attention!

After sundown it was impossible to keep the feet warm. Men sat on their beds with blankets round them trying to read in the comparative darkness, stamped up and down the small courtyard, or adopted Lambert's habit of walking for miles, and then retiring immediately in the hope of sleeping for a few hours. Many patronised the *vino* shops, which were nightly crammed to the doors with a mighty crowd of noisy men who swilled drafts of potent Italian wine as though it were English beer, with remarkable results. At first the wine was delicious, but the demand was so great that sour immature liquid tasting like vinegar soon took its place, and completely upset many a strong stomach.

Coal was unobtainable in Italy from first to last. It cost " umpteen " pounds per ton, and the British used wood, which had to be " scrounged " daily by a fatigue party.

One day, the platoon had chopped down a most suitable tree for log purposes, and were dragging it home in triumph when the old *padrone* of their billet met them. Off went his hat into the air, up went his hands, and a torrent of fluent Italian met them. As usual the flow was met with laughs and humorous remarks, but the old man's attitude was so

HOME COMFORTS AT RAMON

frenzied, that it was evident that his property had been mutilated, and the trunk was reluctantly handed over.

It was a bad start for people living together, and for weeks it was difficult to believe that the old man was not wishing the British to Hades whenever he spoke. The habit of throwing his hat anywhere and everywhere, tearing his hair, rolling his eyes and thundering out a mass of harsh words, conveyed the impression that he was a violent-tempered brigand, but actually he was quite harmless, and his wild words merely embellished with the energy and fire of the Latin race.

His wife, son, daughter and daughter-in-law lived in the cottage, with a little crowd of children, and the two men did various jobs while the women tended to the house and meals. Once or twice during the day maize cobs and twigs were lighted on the huge fireplace, and a simple meal of macaroni soup and *polenta* served. Immediately it was over the whole crowd adjourned to the cowshed, which was highly odorous but decidedly warm. Under an oil lamp the whole lot sewed and chatted and recited a Litany each night before retiring.

Air raids were frequent and violent. Enemy airmen bombed Treviso and Castlefranco frequently, and the family would wander about frenziedly, wringing their hands and murmuring, "*Christo!*" or "*Sanctisima Maria*," while the soldiers did their best to reassure them. This usually took the form of patting them consolingly, and shouting, "Courage-o!" or "Patience-o!"

Bitter cold gradually drove the British into the cowshed, and before many days had passed, one or two men were always to be found in the family circle, which included two oxen, two calves and a sow. They succeeded in making themselves understood, although attempts to speak the language convulsed the natives, who wisely did not attempt English.

Mutual distrust faded rapidly. Any unused (or unwanted) portion of the men's food was a welcome addition to the Italian larder, while the use of the scanty fire for toast-making made a goodly return.

There was genuine sympathy with the folk in a series of minor tragedies. A cow gave birth to a calf, and a sow delivered a litter of pigs, but all the infants died. A splendid draught ox followed suit, and then a year-old calf.

It was a painful series of losses, and at each fresh shock the old man threw his hat into the air, tore his white locks and howled, tears ran down the women's cheeks, and the British looked on with grave faces. However, before the bodies were cold, they were skinned and cut up. Gory heads, huge chunks of meat, and pools of congealed blood obstructed the path to the loft, and the British ate their food with the ensuing smell added to other odours. A large number of brigands visited the house, and not before a dozen Italians had screamed, gesticulated and shrugged shoulders at one another for hours, were the carcases removed. Lice caused agonies during this period. They had bred a large quantity on the journey, and the lack of clean clothing, or baths, had helped the horrible parasites to find ideal quarters. Every day crowds of soldiers stripped to the waist, stood in the snow, removing the pests in dozens. Frozen feet were preferable to that intolerable irritation.

Only one man in the whole battalion seemed impervious to the attacks of the little beasts, a bluff, splendid-tempered boat-owner, named Harrington, and the reason for his immunity became tragically apparent in a very short time.

Among these delightful surroundings, the platoon lived, dined and slept. It was useless to complain. The officers were fresh and not familiar with the men, and with nice beds, servants to do all the work and to prepare tasty meals four times a day, it was

HOME COMFORTS AT RAMON

probably hard for them to believe that the men were uncomfortable.

Christmas brought the terribly delayed mail, plenty of smokes and the promise of a Gargantuan feast, and the soldiers' hearts were unusually light as they marched down the frosty road towards the banqueting-hall. Every man carried his mug, for beer was free. Every mug was being used as a kettle drum, to accompany marching songs, carols and the old English airs associated with that dear land a thousand miles away.

Roars of laughter and rousing cheers interspersed the songs. "The Mistletoe Bough" was first favourite, with an ever-lengthening emphasis of the last line: "Oh, Oh-h-h-h-h the Mistletoe Bough-wow-wow-wow-wow," ending in a succession of stentorian miaows and cat-calls.

The dinner was to be held in some sort of schoolroom, discernible at a distance by the haze of smoke that overhung it. In an adjacent shack were assembled all the battalion cooks, superintending the roasting of lines of turkeys, suspended over a series of huge wood fires.

All the cooks looked alike. They were normally bank clerks, Government officials, business men or tradesmen, who had drifted into their jobs in some mysterious manner, but to-day they were uniformly greasy, grimy, perspiring black-faced niggers, cooking for hundreds of men in clouds of smoke and profanity, with possibly tender thoughts of the million mothers with similar tasks at home.

Wild cheers broke from the troops at the glorious sight, responded to by the cooks with the waving of the beer mugs that were very necessary items in their outfits.

An extraordinary scene was being enacted at one side of the building. Standing with his back to the wall was the Sergeant-Major. Alert and sharp, with a staccato word of command like a whiplash, he was a man of war, and wore the D.C.M. ribbon. Now he was being put through a course of the easiest manual drill by the company officers.

He appeared to find the matter somewhat difficult. At the word "'Shun" he would pull himself up with a convulsive jerk, stand straight for a second, and then slowly fall back to the wall to the shouts of " Stand fast there ! " " Hold it, that man ! " " Don't let me see an eyelid move ! "

The " Tommies " put the Sergeant-Major through his paces with gusto. All the stern injunctions of barrack-squares came to one mind or another. Shouts of command, howls of criticism, scathing comments on the indifferent obedience to commands, and personal remarks of an unprintable character rang in the ears of the bemused non-com. The men made up a lot of lost ground during those few minutes, and reduced their victim to a palpitating wreck.

They marched cheerily into the schoolroom, which was festooned with boughs of fir trees and the flags of many Allies. It was crowded with long trestle tables and forms, and, wonder of wonders, white tablecloths that produced a round of cheers from the delighted troops.

The men seated themselves in their usual sections, and, while awaiting the feast, were served with their free beer. From some unknown source one produced a huge two-gallon enamelled gallipot, which he insisted upon being filled, swearing with mighty oaths that he would consume the contents before nightfall.

A short interval, and the door opened to admit grimy cooks, and a wonderful smell of poultry. With slight suspicions of staggers, the cooks delivered large turkeys to the different sections, and followed them up with steaming dishes of potatoes and (luxury untold) fresh vegetables.

Shades of Lucullus ! What a meal that was !

HOME COMFORTS AT RAMON

After months of bully beef, stew, rice, sodden masses of bread that brave boys had conveyed under heavy shell fire, to sit before a heaped plateful of Christmas fare was to realise for a brief spell the joys of home.

A tremendous blast on the trombone and the door crashed open. Outside in the cold stood a line of filthy cooks, each bearing aloft a Christmas pudding aflame with spirit. They marched triumphantly round the room to the accompaniment of crashing cheers, and the rattling of spoons and forks on dishes and mugs and appalling blasts from the trombonist.

They were real puddings, prepared and cooked in dear old England, transported on some magic carpet across the stricken land of France, over the Alpine walls to the British Army holding the line against the Austrian hordes.

The smell brought back all those delights which seemed so remote, and which many men felt would never be theirs again. The more boisterous made unearthly rows, bowing before the succulent platefuls, toasting them and making merry jests, but there were sad thoughts behind many a grinning face, and the troops plunged into greater noise and jollity in an endeavour to hide them.

The cooks were brought in two by two, wobbly and sleepy after their exertions and libations, and leaning heavily on one another, while the soldiers danced round them, singing songs of war and peace, accompanied quite unmusically with furious blasts from the enthusiastic trombonist. The popular major appeared in the midst of the uproar, and received a reception which appeared to stagger him by its heartiness and fervour.

Rumour had it that the old soldier, always popular with the men despite a voice of thunder and a vitriolic tongue, had secured a real Christmas dinner for the troops in the face of innumerable difficulties, and whether this was true or not the " Tommies " gave him the credit and cheered him until the roof shook.

It was a glorious two hours in the midst of a long campaign, but there was no further jollification, and in the early afternoon the troops meandered back heavily to their cold billets. Some of them found this task somewhat difficult, and the hero of the giant gallipot, who had carried out his vow, was assisted on either side by two sympathetic companions.

Unfortunately, along the frozen road two officers approached them. Military instinct was strong even on Christmas Day. Pulling themselves together with a mighty effort, they switched their heads round in approved style, and brought their hands to their caps in a smart salute. The salutes must have jerked them off their balance for the lot fell with a crash in a confused heap, while the officers hurried by with averted heads. The gallipot hero wished to remain lying on the road, and it took an hour of consistent entreaty and energy to save him from being frozen to death.

Replete with the unaccustomed food and drink, it was a matter of some difficulty to climb the steep ladders leading to the miserable billets, but, this feat accomplished, the men wrapped themselves in blankets and subsided into slumber, while the light faded slowly, and the icy blasts from the mountain grew steadily colder and colder.

Thoughts of cheerful, fire-lit homes came to Lambert lying with eyes staring into the gloom—visions of fair-haired wife and romping boys roasting chestnuts and pulling crackers.

Christmas was celebrated in great style by all battalions in the Brigade. Many tales came from surrounding villages. A kilo away in Poggiana, a platoon of the Manchesters painted an old sow with *vino*, and poured quarts of the strong wine down her willing throat until she could not stand, but revolved on her back trying to catch her tail. The owner wandered about with an axe for days after, trying to discover the culprit. Other stories came from the Warwicks and Gordon Highlanders, and evidently traditions had been well maintained in the latter regiment.

Paternal feelings in Lambert prompted an interest in the Italian "bambino." They were jolly little kids, attired in the most extraordinary costumes, but there was an appalling amount of skin disease among them.

With Bright, he tackled the baby of the household, whose face was covered with nasty sores. Together they journeyed to a distant village, and after a prolonged struggle with the pharmacopœia found the Italian equivalent for white precipitate powder. Armed with this, they gave instructions to the grateful mother, which consisted of energetic gestures and the most dreadful mixture of personal pronouns and nouns conceivable.

"*Bambino impetigo*," stuttered Lambert. "*Mio amico farmacista Londra. Ecco precipitato podire bianco.*"

The reader can judge the wonderful strides the man had made in the language by the following translation: " Baby impetigo. My friend London chemist. Here white precipitate powder."

Over a month was spent in all kinds of training at Ramon. The Austro-German offensive had been stopped at the river Piave, and the wintry weather had made operations in the mountains impossible.

However, orders to move came at last, and the battalion packed. As the platoon left the billet the women burst into tears, the old Italian threw his hat into the air, tore his scanty locks, kissed every man he could catch, and waved violent farewells, while tears rolled slowly down his lined cheeks.

CHAPTER IV

NERVESA

GIAVERA was the first of the evacuated villages to be reached, and the retreating Italians had converted it into a huge marine store. Uniforms, rifles, ammunition and equipment littered the whole place. Ditches and dykes were chock full of dirty underclothing, puttees, shrapnel helmets, tin cans and every conceivable kind of equipment.

The British had to clear up most of it, and how they hated it. Any feeling they had against their allies during the long residence, was caused by the Italian lack of the most elementary sanitary principles, and for our men to have to continually " fug " areas of filth roused feelings of bitter resentment that did not lessen in time, but grew stronger.

After Ypres, the road leading to the lines was comparatively leafy and rural, but the Austrian guns had made havoc of the villages. They were deserted, and prominent buildings lay in ruins. Campaniles were piles of bricks, or jagged portions of them stood out against the skyline. Explosions and columns of black smoke came from the vicinity of the monastery standing on a hill, and some part of it disappeared with each shell.

Nervesa had evidently been a pretty little riverside village, a miniature of Richmond. Elegant châteaux standing in palm-bedecked gardens were still standing, but great holes had been blown in the artistically tinted walls. It was night when the battalions filed

NERVESA

into billets, and little could be seen, but the morning revealed all the details of a great domestic tragedy.

At some recent period, the unfortunate inhabitants had been turned out at a moment's notice. Everything had been left. Furniture still remained in the houses. Pictures hung on the walls. Beds were a tumbled mass of clothing and the remains of meals were still on dining tables. Chests of drawers were full of suits, dresses, prayer-books, photographs, letters and all the intimate paraphernalia of domestic life. It was pitiful to see tiny garments and toys belonging to children lying among the débris.

There had been plenty of looting. Every cupboard and drawer was ransacked, and in many cases the contents turned out in a heap on the floor. In a large château, coats, trousers, dresses and lingerie littered the floor to a depth of several feet. Thousands of sticks of sealing-wax bestrewed a lawyer's office; post office forms flew about in the main street; broken glasses were everywhere in a wineshop, the alms boxes in a tiny chapel in the piazza were shattered and empty, while the tabernacle door gaped open on one hinge.

In the soldiers' billets the floors were carpeted with mattresses four inches thick with mud.

Barbed wire and sandbag defences ran along the river front, where doubtless the peaceful citizens had strolled in happier times. Deep trenches were partly dug, in and out of houses that faced the rushing water, and the British laboured daily for long hours to strengthen them. It was hard work digging the tenacious mixture of clay and stone, and there was a decided tendency on the part of the houses and trenches to collapse, so thousands of doors were removed from the houses, and used for "revetting" the sides, and these reduced the subsidences.

The enemy were fairly quiet and satisfied themselves with "strafing" our artillery positions, and removing buldings in prominent positions that they considered (not without reason) were good observation posts.

There were many alarms. Heavy bombardments were expected several times, and when the Italian Intelligence reported that the town was to be razed to the ground, the troops promptly repaired to dug-outs.

Heavy rain had flooded them and for two hours the British stood in inky darkness, in water up to their knees. A week of horror seemed to pass, and still no unusual sound came from the outside. The advertised hour came and went without incident, and some time later the sodden and frozen men crawled from the muddy holes. They cursed freely, and Lambert was especially sarcastic at the expense of the authorities. His platoon sergeant remonstrated, and there was a bitter exchange of remarks between them.

Lambert had never recovered from his treatment at Meteren, and his tongue lashed out freely at every fresh absurdity, although he knew only too well that outspoken logic does not pay in the Army. On this occasion he little realised how quickly he was to repent of this particular quarrel.

Great care was taken in moving between the billets and trenches. The main street was under observation by the enemy and carefully avoided by the working parties, who made considerable dètours under cover.

One morning, a company commander strolled casually down the street above the trench, gazing over the river towards the enemy lines. As the working party filed out his neglect of the rule was the subject of discussion. He would have been a casualty in Belgium, and even here it was asking for trouble.

A minute or so later the men piled their picks and shovels under an arch, and Lambert was just about to do so, when the world blew up. There was a thunderous roar and everything went dark. An acrid smell filled his nostrils, heavy objects rained upon him, and he fell against the wall with a great gulp of horror.

" My God," ran the thought. " I'm buried alive."

The black void faded to grey, and as the light grew stronger, Lambert realised that he was not dead, and that the smooth ground had been replaced by a great heap of bricks and masonry, from which rose muffled groans. A poor fellow, mortally wounded, groaned at his feet.

"Are you hurt, old boy?" Lambert gasped.

"Yes! Yes! My poor back! Oh! my back!"

Half buried in a heap of débris were several other companions, dead white with dust and staring dazedly into the misty gloom. Almost in the garden lay the sergeant, pitifully still, with a dreadful wound in the head. From the heap rose the sickening fumes of chemicals.

Stretcher-bearers came rushing in, and Lambert, unconscious of injuries, climbed over the wreckage and rejoined his comrades, who stood in a group, with sombre faces.

They eyed him strangely, and he grinned feebly and inquired the reason. They gave none, but one of them hurried him into the aid post, where he subsided into a chair, sick and faint, unconscious of the fact that he was as white as a miller from head to foot, that a vivid stream of blood was running down his ghastly cheek from a gash under the eye, and that another was staining his collar at the back of his neck. His tin hat was dented, and something had smashed a hole in his rifle-butt, ricochetted through his tunic, and bumped violently into a rib.

They brought in a mournful procession a little later. The platoon sergeant, Corporal "Lottie" bleeding and crumpled, and a private with his back riddled like a sieve. Two of Lambert's friends followed tbe stretchers, and one of them was hearty and bluff Harrington, who looked twenty years older as he sat with his head askew, awaiting his turn for attention. Evidently in the shock of the explosion, something had suggested gas, for his mask hung on his chest, crumpled and bloody.

The Austrians had lost no time in registering on the point reported by their observer, and had put a shell into that main street.

CHAPTER V

IN HOSPITAL

Men came into the gloomy room, gazed for a second, and fled precipitately, glad of the darkness outside. There was a more sorrowful look on the veteran Major's face than Lambert had ever seen before. Officers whispered inquiries of the less seriously wounded, then crept out on tiptoe, as the doctor looked up with a helpless expression.

In a great attack casualties are so numerous that the details concerning each are swamped in the flood, but in isolated tragedies all thoughts are focussed on the few.

The platoon sergeant, lying inert with his head open to the air, was one of the most popular men in the battalion. He shone on the football field, and his splendid baritone voice had delighted everybody. Smart on the parade ground, genial with all, and he had been wounded three times before. The private was moaning in agony, his back perforated. "Lottie" was paralysed, and could only use his head and right arm. They asked him if he were comfortable.

"No, I'm not," he snapped in his Cambridge accent. "I'm bloody cold."

Down at the advanced dressing station, the wounded were inoculated against lockjaw, except the serious cases, who were rushed down to the Casualty Clearing Station immediately, and then too late to save the private, who died as they lifted him out of the ambulance.

IN HOSPITAL

Harrington was semi-conscious as the dresser leant over to puncture him. The needle would not go in, and an onlooker advised a new one.

"Should be all right," said the R.A.M.C. orderly. "Did the others."

He fitted a fresh needle, felt the point, and dipped it into the anti-tetanus concoction, but a prick had no effect on Harrington's skin, and the dresser had to use force before the injection could take place.

"This chap hasn't got a skin," he said in astonishment. "It's hide. Bet the lice don't worry him much."

Istrana was the home of pain, and incidentally an important rail-head, where tons of supplies for the Italian E.F. arrived daily. The 24th C.C.S. was in a château, where the large rooms had been converted into wards. Casualties and sick, on arrival, were supplied with handsome chintz bags for their small valuables, their equipment (if any) and clothing taken from them, and they were put to bed after a comforting drink of hot cocoa.

There was a strange medley of men with every kind of complaint or wound in the C.C.S., and never did human nature display its thousands of facets more than in those hospitals behind the lines. Men in agony lay and laughed. Others, with minor injuries, cursed and groaned. Some would have given their last cigarettes to an enemy, and a few would have stolen the false teeth from the mouth of their dying grandmother, but the majority behaved in the usual philosophic "come-day-go-day" manner common to the British soldier.

"Squibs," a lank uncouth youth with large (but very useful) boils on various parts of his anatomy, eked out a precarious existence by combining a little sweeping in the morning, and running errands to the adjacent canteen during the rest of the day. He remained in hospital by the one service, and obtained a commission of cigarettes, chocolates and other delectable commodities by the other.

The " Old 'Un " hobbled about in slippers and a civilian waistcoat which he absolutely refused to part with, and the prolonged laugh of a giant sergeant from the Artillery could be heard throughout the building, infecting everybody and making them laugh at the unknown joke. Those homes of suffering were incubators of stories and jokes. Quite a large proportion of the men had years of service to their credit, and their tales varied from the breathless to the screamingly comic.

The smart of healing wounds, and the weakness that resulted from the terrible shock, were forgotten when the veteran fighter related his worst attack of wind-up, when he half-crossed the bridge over the Ypres canal seven times, to bolt back like a rabbit each time, only regaining his nerve after two hours scuttling to and fro; or when the big Artillery sergeant described how the British saved all their guns in the terrible retreat from Caporetto, alternately aided by Italian tractor drivers, with revolvers at their heads, or three hundred volunteers who dragged the heavy guns for miles.

Even when reciting the most strenuous or perilous passages, the gunner punctuated every few sentences with his prolonged and hearty laugh. It fascinated Lambert, who was to encounter it in bizarre circumstances later on. There were *other* stories, which provoked howls of laughter from all except Harrington who did not appear to hear, but lay for hour after hour with half-closed eyes. Rumour had it that nearly a year later he would jump violently at the slightest sound. Modern shells are not good for the nervous system.

There was a change of orderlies one week, and a youthful corporal tried to get " walking cases " up at the proper time, instead of five minutes before

IN HOSPITAL

breakfast. With prods and shouts he exhorted the patients to "show a leg," "rise and shine," etc., etc. After a few minutes of the noise, several old hands sat up and looked at him, and then proceeded to curse him, his family, relations and ancestors back to Adam. When one finished, another commenced, and it was an education in Army language and invention. The youth fled, to worry no moore.

Only the Army authorities in Italy know the reason why two hospitals were placed near the large rail head and why a third should have been constructed close-by. It made the journey to the train shorter for the poor maimed fellows booked for England, but they had to be lifted into ambulances for the few hundred yards to be covered, when a mile or two would have made no difference, and they would have been saved the horror of nightly air raids, which were presumably intended for the stores of war material, but were just as likely to hit the hospitals.

Night after night, the wounded and sick lay and listened to the whirr of the aeroplanes, the thud of the anti-aircraft guns, and the sickening crash of bombs. They lay and writhed in mental torture, or discomfort, as the whirring came nearer and nearer, and as this usually commenced at tea-time, and continued at intervals during the night, the suspense was long drawn-out.

The man next to Lambert had managed to secrete a tin hat under his bed, and directly the raiders were within hearing, he donned it with a deep groan, which was usually the first of a long series. He had been wounded by the same shell, and there were many fierce arguments between the two men. Lambert held that proximity to death lessened fear, and the counter-argument was that it increased it. The point was never settled satisfactorily and the groaning continued.

Most of the men remained in bed during the attacks,

but the "Old 'Un" invariably put on his civilian waistcoat, and shuffled about the building all night.

No bombs hit the dump, but one dropped outside the hospital, shaking all the beds violently, and sending showers of glass over their occupants. Another dropped in the middle of the men constructing the new C.C.S., and the R.A.M.C. had twenty-four of their comrades brought in, bleeding and mutilated. One of them was suffering from "bomb-shock" and his convulsive jerks, day and night, were distressing to watch.

Lambert's slight wounds were nearly healed by this time, and the desire for action prompted him to wander round the district. The garden was beautiful, but it was too confined, and the entire absence of letters from home and a lack of money produced a restlessness that made the boundaries of the hospital much too small. It was an offence to leave the grounds, but that mattered little.

His platoon sergeant was lying in the other C.C.S. and Lambert called in the hope that a familiar would be welcome. Permission to see the poor fellow was readily accorded, but the report was too much. The wounded man had never recovered consciousness. In his delirium he had sung so continuously and loudly that removal to a marquee had been imperative, and his favourite song had been "Old Soldiers Never Die." Several operations had been unsuccessful and his case was absolutely hopeless. Lambert turned and left the building.

Back at the hospital his companion was very busy. They had asked him to do a little job, and for some hours he had been swabbing indiarubber sheets, which came down from the operating theatre in quick succession as the victims of the previous night's raid were dealt with!

That night Lambert walked quietly down to the side entrance, with the intention of having a little

IN HOSPITAL

ramble in the dark. A bright light in a little room near the exit attracted his attention. It came from a powerful acetylene lamp that carved a brilliant blue arc out of the blackness, focussing two hands that held a white object possessing a vividly red end. It was a human foot !

Lambert turned sick and hurried back to the ward.

"Had enough of this," he announced. "I'm going back to the 'batt.'"

CHAPTER VI

"WIND-UP" AND DOWN

Two out of the five British Divisions had returned to France immediately the Austrian advance was stopped by the flooded Piave. The remaining three were allotted a sector, and hard work on the Montello covered the doings of the Honourable Artillery Company for a number of weeks.

They cut down entire coppices of brushwood for conversion into revetments for trenches, spent night after night digging great underground chambers in deep hollows of the Montello, mounted guard many a night over the icy Piave, and dug, unmolested, a deep defence trench in full view of the enemy, until he decided to create a diversion with a few dozen shells.

The Montello abounded in tremendous holes, and in one, that was at least one hundred feet deep, reposed the company cookhouse. "Mess orderlies" had to descend into the bowels of the earth three times daily, and ascend again with the company's meals. A large dixie of food is never light at the best of times, and to bring one up fifty deep steps, narrow and slippery, required every ounce of a man's strength, and invariably covered him with stew, tea or greasy soot. Of all the unmentionable cookhouses in hundreds of places, the one in the Montello stands out as the most fearsome.

Orders came to move when the vines were beginning to sprout, and on the first day's march a word ran round from man to man along that long column: "*France!*" Nobody knew where it came from, but it flew like quicksilver from the head of the line to the transport bringing up the rear.

" France ! France ! ! France ! ! ! "

What horrible visions that one short word conjured up ! Each man had seen, or heard, the wealth of horror that it signified, and a very dispirited battalion trudged along those weary miles.

It might not have been his fault, but everybody blamed the officer, who was temporarily in command, for the next day's doings. He was a tall, loud, self-opinionated, conceited captain and was cordially hated for some indefinable reason—possibly for the veiled threat that invariably issued from a smiling face, or the recurrence of the personal pronoun " I." He used to speak of having learned to love the company he commanded, and in return they had learned to detest him wholeheartedly.

The march started in the middle of the morning and lasted for over five hours. There was no food *en route*, no halt except the regulation ten minutes per hour, and the horror of continuous tramping on an empty stomach with full pack would tax the powers of a famous writer to describe.

Lambert was in particular trouble. He had left his boots for repair some days previously, and after several visits had found the bootmakers packed for moving and a new pair left for him. It did not take long for the leather to draw his feet, and after a couple of hours the flesh was inflamed and painful to a degree. The remaining three hours were æons of agony.

The acting commanding officer took the salute at the entrance to a small village. Lambert snarled like a dog as he passed the tall figure, and a large percentage of the troops did not hesitate to mutter curses. They crossed the river and filed into a huge warehouse, dumped their belongings, and limped out into the village, full of wrath and desperation. The French troops were in the district, and a wine shop was stocked to the doors with all kinds of liquor.

In a very short time it was filled to overflowing and the men drank everything they could buy, as fast as it could be served. The effect of cognac, vermouth or wine on tired frames and empty stomachs did not matter a jot. They had finished a dreadful day. They were going to France to be killed. " Drink, drink, and be merry, for to-morrow we die ! "

Saturnalia reigned in that little village. Men staggered along the dark lanes singing at the tops of their voices, waving bottles in the air. Others danced on the tables in the wineshop, which rocked with the babel of shouts and songs and the pounding of heavy boots. Nobody wanted to eat. Give the dinner to the pigs ! It was too late now ! " Le's have another bo'l."

Fortunately the march next day was not so prolonged, but the libations continued for several days, while preparations were being made to entrain. The tall captain ordered a parade and lectured the men. He started very well, and had he left off in the middle much good might have resulted, but the inevitable threat appeared and companies marched off the field singing :

> " Here's to good old wine,
> Drink it down my boys ! "

A ditty of many voices, eulogising most forms of liquor, and the drinking continued during every interval of packing for the Western front.

At last kits were packed, and men were sitting on them waiting for the hour for parade. The advance party had gone to the station, the cookers were in the train, limbers were on the trucks, and now nothing remained but the march to the station, and then away for muddy, gory, France.

The appointed time passed, and another hour crept

"WIND-UP" AND DOWN

by. Conversation lapsed and men looked at one another solemnly. What did it mean ? The usual Army delay or——? Another hour crawled by, and still there was no move.

Suddenly a shout from below and an excited soldier pounded into the billet.

" Washed out ! Washed out ! " he howled.

Men danced and sang, shook hands with one another, charged about like bulls, formed a ring and danced round madly, and, when breathless, subsided on to packs and searched for bread and cheese. It was the first time the lack of transport facilities had saved the 7th Division from an addition to their record of thirty-seven months on the Western front, but not the last.

Rumour followed upon rumour, and glorious news took the place of gloomy tidings. The H.A.C. were going to do " guards " at Headquarters. From now onward they would view horrid war from the comparative safety of the " base." No more hefty digging, cruel treks, or the appalling scream of approaching shells. Avaunt fear of sudden death or bleeding wounds ! Those terrors were things of the past. They were to move immediately to Utopia.

After the polishing of every buckle and square inch of leather, the battalion started off, and every song in an extensive repertoire resounded along the white roads. For hour after hour the troops went from one chorus to another, and the distressing length of the march did not damp their joy. It might be the last long walk !

The men stumped cheerfully up the steep, winding hill leading to a pass that would have been a fiendish ending on an ordinary occasion, and subsided on to their hard couches after one of their longest marches with spirits on a high level.

Disillusion came in the morning. With expressions of regret the wonderful news was denied. There had been a misunderstanding and the battalion had been ordered to Galzignano for a course of mountain-fighting. All the Division were coming in turn.

It was a cruel blow and did not make the new form of training any easier. Galzignano was a jewel: a struggling collection of châteaux, with lovely gardens nestling in a valley surrounded by vine-covered, wooded hills, with a number of well-stocked cafés, where the troops could eat and drink in comfort.

Towering over the village was the steep height of Monte Rua, scarred with tracks through the woods and surmounted by a picturesque monastery, where the monks meditated and tended their gardens with a lovely vista of Italian scenery beneath them.

Up and down these steep heights and winding tracks, the British climbed and scrambled, practising attack and defence in the continuous sunshine. It was desperate work for the lungs and muscles to [men used to the plains and pimples of Britain. Although very early spring, the days were warm and cloudless, and many of the stunts seemed more fitted to goats than men, but the troops " stuck it," as they endured anything, and when the disappointment of crushed hopes had subsided, there remained the consolation of plenteous eggs, fruit and wine awaiting them in the village nestling below.

Lambert spoilt his sojourn in the nicest billet they had had for months. From the rifle range one morning, platoons were ordered home separately, and were to climb over the mountain top and down the other side by any track they could find. In charge of a youthful corporal, with the wind and strength of a horse, the platoon dashed up the precipitous slope at a pace that soon left the elder men behind.

He scrambled upwards at his best rate, with every muscle aching and his breath coming in short and painful gasps, but the remainder had disappeared. A long climb up the steep road to the monastery had no result and Lambert, surveying the patchwork of country

"WIND-UP" AND DOWN

stretching before him thousands of feet below, picked out a track leading to the village and plunged downhill towards it.

He had descended several hundred feet when the platoon emerged from a coppice high above him, and the corporal, full of newly-gained authority, ordered him to join them, and repeated the command when that individual pointed out that their paths would eventually meet.

Aching with fatigue, and remembering with annoyance General Foch's statement that a wise General marches at the pace of his slowest man, Lambert refused, consigned the corporal to torrid regions on a repetition of the command, and sat on a rock to await the others.

He was "run" for failing to comply with the orders of an N.C.O., and, feeling too proud to defend and too wise to argue with the regulations which always convicted the "men," spent a week's C.B. in a corner of the billet, while his friends enjoyed the unaccustomed luxuries in various parts of the district.

During this period he slept on a bed for the first time for nearly a year. A small room adjoined the large hall in which the men slept, containing a four-poster with a large spring mattress. One night Lambert quietly wrapped himself in his blanket, laid on the yielding springs, and turned and tossed in an uneasy slumber throughout the night.

He earned quite a reputation for generosity by positively insisting upon a comrade indulging in the luxury the following night, and, in his turn, this man absolutely refused to be so selfish as to occupy the room for two nights running.

Just over a fortnight's "intensive training" was deemed sufficient to accustom the troops to mountain-fighting, and one fine morning the battalion commenced a long trek towards the Asiago Plateau.

CHAPTER VII

MULES!

"ME!" said Lambert. "Never been on a horse in my life."

"Nor I," came the chorus from several men.

"Well, why are we detailed?"

"Probably for the reason that we know nothing about it."

The Dolomite Alps rose like a mighty wall outside the little town. They were some miles away, but in the clear atmosphere appeared to spring up from the ground just at the back of the houses. White peaks peered over one another's shoulders as far as the eye could see, both forward and to right and left.

Twenty men waited in a little group in the corner of a large yard littered with wagons and harness. They had been detailed to take charge of a similar number of new mules, which were expected at any moment from the railway station.

Few of the men knew anything about horses, or even harness, and none had any experience of mules.

The transport sergeant gave them a few interesting details. Mules could kick in about ninety-seven different ways, combining in one animal the vices of most four-footed beasts; if they could not kick they would bite, and if both were impossible, would try and roll on their objective. They were as strong as lions and timid as mice. Would eat anything from barbed wire to telegraph poles, and were dirty in their habits. After this promising opening the talk swerved on to harnessing, grooming, and watering, and the novices' minds were soon a confused tangle of surcingles, pack saddles, gullet straps, and so on.

It was a hurried lecture and each man was supposed to know all about it, but there were doubtful looks as a string of animals came through the gateway, led by the regular transport man. They were enormous brutes, with coats of all colours. All their ears were set well back, nostrils were distended, and great eyes rolled in their sockets.

They were tied up and the sergeant strolled up to make their acquaintance. A pair of heels just missed his stomach and he retreated hurriedly, watched by the mule, who had twisted his head round and appeared to be smiling all over his face.

The new squad were lined up; strong bass brushes were handed to them, and the sergeant, walking along the line of heads, allotted a beast to each man, with instructions to groom them.

It was one thing " to go over the top," or keep a stiff lip during heavy shelling, but quite another to plunge into a confused mass of whinnying animals whose kicks meant casualties.

However, if soldiers had hesitated at risky jobs half of them would have been shot for cowardice, so into the crowd went the " muleteers " with fear in their hearts, and words of endearment on their lips. They kept at as respectable a distance from the hoofs as possible while brushing muddy coats with the professional " shish-shish "; but the animals were too close to allow much room, and men jumped out at frequent intervals as their animals formed acrobatic feats. Most of the mules laid down and rolled in the mud as soon as their coats were reasonably clean.

Feeding and watering were fearsome jobs with mules that jumped and struggled at the slightest noise, but they were comparatively simple compared with harnessing and packing next morning. All the leather straps were perfectly new and stiff, the pack saddles were weighty, and the mules skipped about like kittens. They particularly detested their ears being touched, and as it was impossible to get a bridle on without, the yard was soon full of struggling men and animals. Lambert's beast kept rearing his head in the air, and as it was seventeen hands high, that individual made plaintive inquiries for a step-ladder. He tried to tighten the pack saddle with his hands, but the straps were too stiff, and in desperation he gripped with his teeth and promptly loosened one. Old hands had to force the bits into the tightly clenched teeth of the animals.

A box of ammunition was to be placed on each side of the saddles, and the men were expected to hold the mules with one hand and lift eighty pounds with the other. To leave go of the bridle meant a bolt, and it was impossible to lift the heavy weight otherwise. N.C.O.'s were frenziedly summoned, and helped to lift the boxes on the fidgety animals, who jumped and curveted immediately they felt the weight.

As soon as one box was on, the saddle slipped owing to the mule's gentle habit of blowing out his stomach when being strapped, and relaxing it later, and the tightening process had to be repeated. Some of the beasts refused to have the burden at all; others jumped so furiously that the boxes jolted off the rope loops, and the mules promptly bolted round the yard, dragging a tangled mass of harness and ammunition behind them.

It took several hours to finish the job, and a perspiring, shaken party led their animals out of the yard on the road to the mountain. There were incidents every few minutes. The hoofs of a horse, or clank of a passing motor lorry continually frightened the mules, who would immediately jump into the air, or kick out in every direction, converting the chain into a mass of disconnected links composed of rearing animals, with men hanging frantically to their bridles.

Some men let go, and the animals bolted immediately, followed from a considerable distance by their panting masters, who usually gave up the chase, and waited for the truant to be captured by the mounted sergeant. It was awkward when the mule dashed down the steep sides of the mountain road, and stopped a hundred yards below to eat a succulent bush or young tree, or when the saddle slipped, and the men were faced with the necessity of collecting a mule, two boxes of ammunition, and pieces of harness from various parts of Italy.

Occasionally, mules refused to turn corners, and stood stock still, trembling with fright, impeding the progress of the mile-long Divisional train. It was useless to tug and pull, as a mule with firmly planted feet is about as easy to move as a steam roller, consequently, human deceit was the only remedy and the animal had to be gently led back the wrong way, a circle described at an opportune moment, and the journey resumed. Lambert got a mile behind on one occasion, when his animal kept stopping to hee-haw a prolonged lament for the distant shores of his Barbary home.

The way led ever upwards, along the wonderful mountain roads cut out of the cliff face. The lovely Italian plains grew smaller and smaller as the transport gradually ascended, until they resembled a patch-work quilt of many colours. But the muleteers were in no mood to admire beauty. Even at halts they dared not leave go of their burdens, who were startled every few minutes, while the animals chewed any bush, fence, or chunk of mud that took their fancy. After eight hours of decidedly steady climbing, the procession turned into a field, and, after feeding and watering, the brutes were tied up and the men could rest their aching limbs and tired brains.

It was always animals first in the Army. Men were

cheap, so it was of little consequence that there was no sleeping accommodation for them.

Lambert had managed his mule fairly successfully, although its super-sensitiveness was very trying, but he had not experienced the joy of a chase. It was not to be denied him ! After hours of walking on the second day, a halt was called for food, and with the confidence begat of desperation, Lambert tied his " moke " to a telegraph post, and after placing nosebags over a head that reared itself yards high, went off to find something for himself.

After a hasty snack, he returned to make ready for another move. The mule immediately jumped violently, tugged like a being possessed, snapped his bridle and disappeared down the road in a smother of dust. Lambert ran until his heart nearly burst, gasped out thanks to a man who had stopped the truant, and trudged wearily back to the cursing sergeant and laughing comrades.

It grew bitterly cold as they mounted higher, and when the " train " reached a deep hollow dotted with wooden huts, it was to find the rest of the battalion (who had been brought up in motor lorries) vigorously snowballing one another.

The animals were packed tightly on each side of a long shed, where they amused themselves by kicking and biting one another, or any human being that they could get hold of. At feeding times they snapped like wolves, and roared like lions, and in the intervals chewed one another's blankets or the wooden posts supporting the shed, although some became more fastidious in time and spat out nails and buckles.

Italian descriptive writers referred to the Asiago Plateau as the " Plateau of Thirst," and in the first months water was extremely difficult to find. The muleteers had to extricate their animals from the jigsaw puzzle called the horse-lines several times daily, and lead them through thick snow, up a steep hill and

MULES!

down into a hollow where a pool of icy water had collected. Most of the mules evinced a desire on each occasion to plunge into the middle, dragging their masters behind them.

One foggy morning Lambert had got off the mark quickly and was standing on the water's edge, when a large grey beast dashed out of the gloom and plunged into the centre of the pool. Cries for help came from the distance and Lambert dragged his animal down the track. Lying on the snow was one of his companions with a trickle of blood oozing from his mouth. He looked like an actor in a Lyceum drama, but fortunately it was not a serious case. The mule had kicked the man in the chest, causing him to bite his lips, which accounted for the ominous trickle.

Strenuous days followed. After a short rest, frequently broken by long hours of "picket," the mules had to be watered, fed and harnessed, and walked for hours through miles of mountains to the railhead of Campiello, where rations for the battalion awaited them.

On one of the first journeys the "train" took a short cut marked "Muleterra Campiello," which started as a narrow little path, leading through a picturesque pine wood. When too far advanced for retreat the party found that it developed suddenly into a precipitous gully, full of ice and rocks, that literally dived down the mountain side.

Men and mules slid and slipped down the perilous slope. First one fell and then the other. The animals trod on the men's toes, or glissaded yards on their bodies. Men fell, and were dragged over rocks, and through bushes, and the party arrived on the road one mass of bruises and cuts. The longer way via the road was patronised on future occasions.

Campiello "dump" was always thick with mud, in which goods of all kinds had to be extracted from huge stacks, bound with thick ropes in several kinds of intricate knots, and fixed on each side of the mules. The weight had to be more or less equal or the saddle would slip and the burden slide under the animal's stomach, with the result that can be imagined.

All the weights were very great. Boxes of " bully," sacks of oats, bales of fodder, or huge bags of meat were about the same standard, almost too heavy for a strong man to lift, but the muleteers had to accomplish the task—usually with the willing help of the " regulars," and the two hour tramp up the mountain followed.

On one of these occasions, a number of huts built on ledges on the mountain side was pointed out to Lambert as the next billet of the battalion. Quite near was a notice : *Tenere la destra,* which the private advised his friends was the name of the spot. When they discovered that the words meant " Keep to the right " he did not hear the last of the matter for many a long day.

It was desperately hard work, that started early and ended late, and the comforts were none. Sleeping apartments were odorous and draughty adjuncts to the stable, where the nostrils were titivated by the aroma, and sleep disturbed by the stamping and fighting animals.

The regular transport men did their best for the novices, who appreciated to the full the unselfish, merry, and altogether splendid lot of fellows they had joined. Lambert contracted another of those Army friendships that were so tragically transitory in too many cases. Wraybury was a tall, self-possessed man, about his age, similarly circumstanced as to business, wife and family, and they had many interesting chats in their murky billet. They thoroughly agreed on one feature of the new life. The job was not worth having, but the transport did not mean the front line trenches. There was a wealth of comfort in that thought !

Twelve men out of the twenty were paraded a few days later, and returned to their companies as not being strong enough ; Lambert was one of them. Wraybury remained, and died a month or two later from a kick in the face.

Muleteers followed one another in quick succession. Few were strong enough, but they had to do. Some of the " mokes " became really useful animals, others remained incorrigible. Two were put into harness in a limber, bolted down one of the steepest roads, nearly succeeded in killing the driver, who had a perilous journey on the centre pole, and quite succeeded in respect to one of themselves.

At this period little was known in the British Empire regarding the Italian Expeditionary Force. It was a " side show," but the British set about their sector of the Asiago Plateau in characteristic fashion. Along the steep mountain roads that commenced at Monte Pau, and continued for three or four miles in several directions, there were only clusters of wooden huts dotted about the rocky slopes. There was not a house, shop, woman or child in the many square miles of snow-clad mountain and forest, and the accommodation for soldiers was of the scantiest.

Water for horses and men came chiefly from pools ; trees for fuel had to be cut down, and sawn up by amateurs ; there was little accommodation for horses, and the men crowded together on shelves in leaky huts like so many bales of merchandise.

A month or two and the change was wonderful. Miles of water pipes were laid, with taps and troughs at convenient distances. Motor tanks conveyed water to awkward spots. Wood was sent up regularly in rations, and infantry battalions constructed stone roads and horse lines while " at rest."

The water was valuable at that height, and the principal taps were guarded by Italian soldiers. A huge Gordon Highlander, driving a water cart, drove up one morning and greeted the sentry in Italian with a decidedly Gaelic accent.

"*Buon giorno,*" he stuttered, "*Aqua ?*"

"And for what are ye wanting water ? " replied the Italian, in equally broad accents. The Gordon nearly fell off his seat, and gasped out an inquiry.

"Dinna ye ken that I was born in Glesga' ? " was the unexpected reply.

Our artillery brought up crowds of guns, and literally hung them on hooks on the mountain side. Some of the positions were so sheer that lorries had to dump supplies of shells on the road, to be carried up the steep paths by infantrymen.

Peculiarly enough, Division did not call on the battalion nearest the batteries, but those miles away, and the H.A.C. trudged through the mountains for hours, spent the day carrying hundred pound shells over the rocks, with six-inch "Hows" roaring in their ears at intervals, and then marched wearily back along the snowy roads.

"You are the first men to carry our shells," a big R.G.A. gunner told them one day, but the statement did not alleviate the bitterness felt by the infantry. There was no job too long, too filthy, or too dangerous for them and the belief that the French, Italian and German armies employed Labour Companies for rough work, leaving the infantry to die only, intensified the feelings.

Sunday was naturally the same as any other day, and indeed many a hefty "fatigue" or trek commenced on the day of rest. The feelings of the Church were put very tersely by a padre who met a party marching to construct horse-lines on a Sunday morning. It was a job involving much draining of urine and digging of horse manure.

"What's on," he asked the officer, doubtless thinking of his service.

"Horse-standing."

"Good God!"

Naturally the practice of religion was most difficult. Services were impossible in the front line, and Faith had to be expressed by inward prayers at intervals. Grace at meals seemed to be quite inappropriate when thankfulness was non-existent, and morning and night prayers were anachronisms when night and day blended into one period of interminable time.

Down in the valleys there were Catholic churches in every village, and always devout Anglicans were to be found visiting them for their devotions, while the popular little H.A.C. "choirmaster" obliged on many occasions by playing the organ for Benediction with skill and sympathy. Lambert was the surviving Roman Catholic in his company, and, whenever possible, was solemnly inspected by his sergeant-major and despatched to hear Mass offered by the Brigade Padre in the most convenient church, garden, or cattle shelter in the district. On these occasions all the soldiers were regarded as sinless, and received the consolation of the Holy Eucharist without having observed the essentials of fasting and confession.

The infantry became a jack of all trades for several weeks. They helped to improve the "dumps," construct roads and horse-lines, clear the snow with a huge snow plough, and other jobs too innumerable to mention. They had moved to Bussibolo, where huts were built on rock shelves up a mountain whose outer slopes faced the enemy lines. At intervals shells screamed over the top and played havoc with the billets. The shrapnel effect of shells on the rocks of Italy was twenty per cent. greater than on the Western front, and each explosion sent up a tremendous shower of rocks and stones.

Shells expedited work in surprising ways. The cookhouses were well below the road and the fetching of food meant goat-like scrambling up and down the slippery paths—a hateful job. Lambert and a companion were toiling up the road with a heavy load between them when a shell burst a short distance away. Lumps of metal and stones rained on them and they jumped forward as though galvanised. Another scream and they went down the precipitous path like a couple of stags, and landed in the cookhouse in a confused medley of men, dixie and water, just as the crash came !

Shortly after, a smart car toiled up the road containing the Prince of Wales, who was endeavouring to cover an expansive yawn with his gloved hand !

For some unknown reason, the infantry supplied extra guards to the machine guns, and for two nights each platoon stamped about in the ice and snow on a mountain top, and for two days tried to sleep in covered alcoves in the rocks on floors composed of sharply pointed flints, floating in water that dripped from the rough tarpaulin roofs.

One morning, shortly after a British plane had flown over the enemy lines, dropping large quantities of Viscount Northcliffe's propaganda leaflets, and attracting a prolonged spell of anti-aircraft fire, a machine-gunner felt an irritation in the thigh. He rubbed it, but that was painful, and, genuinely puzzled as to the reason, he examined his leg, and found to his astonishment a bullet neatly embedded in the flesh. There were not many cases of men being wounded in this way without knowing all about it at the instant of impact !

After making themselves generally useful for a week or two, the battalion moved up into reserve. They occupied wooden huts perched on either side of a woody gorge full of huge boulders, with a stream zig-zagging down the centre.

Men packed into the huts like sardines. There was just enough room to sit down, and it was not possible to stand upright as there was an upper tier holding a similar jam of men. The awful accumulation of equipment, packs, haversacks, "trench stores," etc., had to be hung everywhere and anywhere, and the soldiers crawled about on all fours like so many animals.

The only light during the long hours of darkness came from candles stuck in all manner of holders, constructed from bully beef tins and similar receptacles. Candle greese dripped on the blankets, tunics or caps, and during mealtimes howls emanated at frequent intervals from unfortunates on the ground floor who had received boiling tea, or hot stew, spilt on the floor above.

It rained, hailed, sleeted and snowed almost without cessation for three weeks, and the roofs gave up the attempt to keep the moisture out after a few hours. Little streams, in dozens of places, fell upon the mugs and tins beneath. The catching of the drips became quite an exciting pastime, similar to a slow game of chess. As soon as a good move was made, an attack developed from another quarter, until the supply of tins gave out.

Pools under the "bed," wet heads and sodden blankets were the order of the day, and as the stream in the "main street" of the gorge was now a torrent, which had to be crossed numberless times, night and day, boots were always wet. There was no relaxation of any kind—they were miles deep in the forest—and the men tried to play cards, read and write, or talk miserably of the time when the war would be no more.

It seemed thousands of years away! Germany had attacked fiercely on the Western front, and relations were involved in the awful retreat. Lambert, writhing with the ache of trench fever, felt that the picture had never been so black. Letters from home were despondent, one of his brothers had been wounded and another was reported missing after the Cambrai disaster.

The orderly corporal came in with orders, to which he listened with complete indifference. Suddenly he brisked up like a terrier. His name was down on orders for a course of "bombing" at Centrale.

CHAPTER VIII

UP AND DOWN THE MOUNTAINS

To be detailed for a " course " was always a joy to the British soldier, no matter on which front he was engaged. It meant detachment from the rigours of the front line, or the incessant " fatigues " of rest billets, and transference to the comparative peace of the base. The course of lectures on various man-killing instruments cloaked quiet naps, the hours of duty were fairly short, and left considerable leisure to visit adjacent towns, with their wealth of oranges, nuts and fried eggs.

" Courses " were particularly welcome from the Asiago Plateau. It meant leaving a cloudy expanse of woods and rocks (to say nothing of a war going on) for the sunlit green of fields and vines, and Lambert and his co-fortunates waited for a convenient lorry with feelings akin to trippers in far-away England.

There was no suggestion of walking down the mountain. That energy was reserved for occasions when it was compulsory. Now they were a small party in charge of a non-com., who no more wished to walk than they did, and, despite occasional shells, they waited in the rain until it was possible to clamber into an obliging lorry.

The road to the plains descended steeply for nearly five thousand feet. There were over thirty hairpin bends, and the depth of the precipice on one side was alarming, but the quiet confidence of the driver, tearing down the well-known track, allayed any secret fears,

UP AND DOWN THE MOUNTAINS 141

which were soon forgotten as the beauty of the view increased. Down below stretched a wonderful expanse of country, in which three great rivers appeared like ribbons, running through patchwork quilt of greens and yellows. Here and there were dotted collections of houses with jet black cypresses, and white campaniles, as a contrast to the red roofs and blues and pinks of the walls. Over the whole expanse the sun shone beneficently, reassuring the trippers from cloudland that it still existed.

An hour's fast run and the party reached their destination in Centrale. (Nearly all the villages in this district commenced with the initial C : Centrale, Chippiano, Cornedo, Calvene, Camisino and Carltrano, were all within a short distance, while there was Campiello, Carriola, Cesuna, Cavrari and Canovo at the top of the mountain road.) Here for ten days all was peace, and when the time came to return, the lotus-eaters started back for the regiment with very doleful feelings.

Things were quiet at the front, and lorries were conspicuous by their absence. After a short march the party waited for a lift for some hours without any success, until a few brave, or timid souls suggested climbing the mountain.

The idea was laughed to scorn ; two men were sent back to report to the base, and the rest adjourned to a large canteen, regaled themselves with the inevitable tea and biscuits, and later found considerable sport in a billet occupied by Italian soldiers. Neither could speak the other's language but it was a simple matter to pick up the rules of the gambling games popular with our Allies. Lambert conversed with an ex-corporal. He was " ex " owing to the fact that "he wished to see his house." He had seen it for three months and when he came back he was corporal no longer !

The conversation was a long job. Each, sentence in Italian from Lambert produced a roar of laughter, with a similar result when the Italian essayed English. The latter was particularly amused when he understood that "seeing his house" in the British Army would probably have ended in a firing-party at dawn.

Lorries bound for the mountain top may have passed in scores at this time. Nobody troubled to look for them, and when dusk was drawing in, and the two men had not returned, the inventive corporal was sent to report matters to the Town Major. He returned in triumph with the address of a billet and promise of rations, and the party proceeded thither in triumph. The corporal accepted an invitation to dinner with some Italians and departed, while the rest of the party laughed themselves ill at a string of the most dreadful stories extant, that followed one another in quick succession from various raconteurs.

The two men sent back to report had not returned at a late hour, but, nearing midnight, heavy steps resounded on the stairs of the billet, together with a few raucous noises, doubtless intended for singing, and the truants lurched into the apartment. It was impossible to ascertain the orders they brought. The only news that could be gleaned was that they had met a "charmin' I-ty" in a hostelry, and after spending a short time together had left him under the table. They were very noisy and one man insisted upon sweeping out the room to a vocal accompaniment, but eventually he wilted under the storm of abuse from sleepy soldiers, and subsided on to his rough bed. About two a.m. there was a similar disturbance, when a couple of Italians carried in their guest—the corporal.

News came in the morn. Base-headquarters had ordered the men to report to the battalion the previous day, even if it meant climbing the mountain !—the Town Major sent news of lorries leaving at an early hour, and the party, jaded but merry, clambered into them after keeping the drivers waiting for an hour or two. The battalion were in the front line—they had to

UP AND DOWN THE MOUNTAINS 143

report to the Transport and rejoin their companies at the same time as the rations.

The time these left each day was known, and ergo ! it was necessary to arrive after that time ! Another prolonged stay at an Italian canteen, and a leisurely climb to the transport lines, and the party arrived long after the ration train had left. There were a few anxious moments with the Lieut.-Quartermaster, but eventually sleeping accommodation was found, and next day the men arrived at their destination, having taken three days on an eight hours' journey.

They were met with gloomy looks. "B" Company had made a fierce raid and several men would be seen no more. Thus ended that course, and after a few days' watching and working in the front lines, the battalion were relieved and departed early one morning for the plains.

Troops descending from the Asiago Plateau used one or other of the various mule-tracks, or *muleterra*. These had no hairpin bends, but descended sheer, and consisted of loose lumps of granite. In full pack, the battalion literally slid down for four hours. The only method was to keep the balance, and dig the heels into the shifting stones. It jarred every nerve in the body, upset almost every man's digestion for days, and reduced them to shaking masses of perspiring humanity long before they reached the shady gardens of Camisino.

Much of their distress, however, was forgotten by the sight of the pitiable condition of a Manchester battalion climbing up the same track in full pack. At short intervals they lay on their backs groaning and gasping, their chests heaving with the exhaustion of dying fishes. It was a terrible sight, and the hospital cases were so numerous that British troops were never allowed to climb the mountain in full pack again.

CHAPTER IX

ALMOST A " REST "

THE transition from the Plateau to Camisino almost defies description. The former was drab, rocky and dry, the latter a sunny garden of fruit and flowers nestling on a cliff above a swift torrent. Down below, the River Astico swirled from the mountains in a mass of foam, through a deep gorge verdant with bushes and wild flowers. It seemed to attract the sunrays, which danced in the clear water, and tempted the soldiers to defy Brigade orders which forbade bathing.

Billets were the usual Italian cottages where scorpions were not unknown, but each stood in a shady garden, thick with grass, in which the troops spent all their available time. Eggs and fruit abounded in the village. Wineshops jostled one another, and, to crown the joy, the long-delayed parcel mail came in to provide Gargantuan feasts for all and sundry. It took many limbers to fetch the parcels, and boys with doting parents received dozens or more at once, until the billets resembled marine stores. There were cakes and sweets for breakfast, dinner and tea, plenty to eat, drink and smoke, little work and long afternoons in the grass beneath the trees, reading, talking or gambling.

It was the loveliest period of the beautiful Italian spring, and a large proportion of the battalion slept out of doors. A ground sheet and a blanket or two on the thick grass, and the men lay contentedly in a natural bed, with all the beauties of Nature around

ALMOST A " REST "

them. A canopy of gleaming stars above, sweet perfumes from the flowers and shrubs, the distant noise of the river below, and the gentle rustling of the breeze through the trees, induced pleasant dreams of England and the day when there should be no war. . . . Only now and then the noise like the banging of a door reminded them that it still existed.

An aqueduct that crossed the river Astico at Camisino was in great request by men visiting the villages on the other bank. It saved a long walk, but as the footpath was only a foot wide, several men under the influence of drink tumbled in and were drowned, and an armed guard became necessary.

This was posted for twenty-four hour periods, and consisted of four men, who were excused duty for the following day, and usually seized the opportunity to apply for a pass to some distant town.

Lambert and three friends completed their vigil, and were duly granted permission to visit Schio, reputed to be one of the jolliest little places in the district. It was twelve kilos away, and the party, after climbing the opposite cliff, commenced the long walk along a' white, dusty road, off which the sun's rays jumped in a blinding glare.

They were tired, hot and thirsty within half an hour and it seemed foolish not to ride in one of the Italian lorries that passed frequently. Signals were exchanged with the next few " Fiats " that dashed past, but all the drivers ignored the signs. Consequently, the British devised the plan of stretching across the road, and getting a lift or being run over.

The driver of the first lorry evidently understood the game and accelerated, narrowly missing two of the troops, but the second one stopped with a graceful wave of the hand ánd deposited them at their destination very quickly.

Schio was a charming village nestling at the foot of a tall mountain, which effectually screened it from shells, although bombs were not unknown. It boasted a fine church, plenty of nice shops and buildings and quite a disproportionate number of bars with an extensive assortment of liquor.

It was very hot, and most of the bars were cool owing to the picturesque awnings shading their doors. Consequently, after a scrappy lunch, the " troops " felt that they needed refreshment and shade, and both seemed to be confined to one class of business.

A tour began which lasted for some hours, during which time the corporal indulged a taste for colour by having a differently coloured liqueur each time, and insisting upon inviting some Italian officials to indulge with him. They acceded gracefully, and astonished the British by proposing a toast : " *Viva Americaines.*"

Systematic shopping followed. Perhaps an inspection of shops would be a better description. It consisted of crowding into every shop, inspecting the stock and walking out again. Lambert and the corporal certainly bought pretty pendants for their wives in distant England, and were extraordinarily amused at purchasing them by weight, but with these exceptions the tradesmen did not benefit to any extent.

One of the party became assertive. Although tea was unobtainable in Italy, he bundled his friends into a café and demanded that refreshing beverage. Lambert, to whom was erroneously credited a knowledge of the language, was ordered to depart immediately and purchase something dainty for the tea they could not get.

He obeyed without demur, and after a considerable interval returned with biscuits, sardines, jam and tinned fruits, to find his friends fast asleep, watched from the distance by a couple of scared waitresses.

Lambert's knowledge of Italian was put to a severe test after this complicated meal. Time was flying, and they were faced with the necessity of walking twelve kilos in a couple of hours. It was unthinkable,

ALMOST A "REST"

and the assertive one tackled the driver of a car standing on the plaza in a lingo of his own invention.

"Ride-o. Motor-o. Camisino-o?" he inquired fiercely.

The driver grinned and shook his head, and responded with a stream of fluent Italian which demoralised the assertive one, but he revived and insisted on Lambert translating. Quite foolishly that individual gave his opinion that the car was a mail van, and nobody was allowed to ride in it without the permission of the Post Office officials. Without further ado the unfortunate Lambert was dragged by main force to the chief post office, where he was compelled by blood-curdling threats to interview several influential members of the "poste Italiano."

It was a severe ordeal out of which the British emerged triumphantly, but solely by virtue of the Italian courtesy. The van was not going to Camisino but to Vicenza, many kilos in the wrong direction, but they would telephone the railway company and obtain permission for their distinguished visitors to travel by a train leaving immediately, and would be pleased to send a clerk to guide them to the station.

Half an hour later the trippers were seated on top of a huge pile of logs destined for the mountains. They were very happy. Song followed song, and the assertive one indulged his taste for words ending in "o," with every person that came within view.

There was plenty of opportunity for exercising his gift as the route ran along the main road, with hundreds of billets packed with Italian soldiers, who returned the greetings with clapping and cheers. It was a triumphant journey, capped by a charming incident, when an Italian soldier deftly threw a bunch of roses into their midst as the train steamed past him!

It was an idyllic existence at Camisino for a few days, but it was too good to last. Orders were issued for a reveille at an unearthly hour, and in the dim dawn

the troops practised a formidable " stunt." After a
march of a mile or two up-stream they descended
the steep banks of the river and waded across the icy
rushing water that soaked them to the waist. On
the other side they gathered into piebald sections,
and for some hours advanced, and charged various
spots, which were given the names of famous Scottish
towns.

For several mornings this watery job was repeated,
and at last the *raison d'être* was explained by bloodthirsty young sergeants who seemed to enjoy the task.
On the Asiago the enemy held a ravine called the Val
d'Assa. It was so deep that aerial photographs did
not show the bottom, but it was known that a stream ran
through it. The Brigade were going to attack this,
and several thousand men were going to converge on
two or three steep and narrow mule-tracks leading
down the ravine. It was most probable that the enemy
would resist strenuously, not only with shells and
machine guns, but also with clouds of gas, and there-
fore this scrambling down the precipice would be
executed in gas masks !

It was an alluring prospect of hopeless confusion
and systematic slaughter, which quite obliterated
the enjoyment of the " rest," and feelings can be
imagined when ultimately the order came for an early
start up the mountain.

CHAPTER X

CLIMBING TO THE FRONT LINE

The troops arose in the middle of the night, and commenced their long climb while the stars still shone in the beautiful deep blue sky. The mule-track rose precipitously from the village street, led through the verdant foothills, and up towards a mighty crag that was so vast that it was plainly visible in the starlight, although five thousand feet high.

An hour of steady climbing and the men were strung out in a great chain ; the head of the battalion hundreds of feet above the rearguard. Another hour and the men dropped down on the stony track for a rest, their faces running with perspiration, and chests heaving with exertion.

It became lighter during each leaden minute of the third hour. Every man's tunic was open at the neck, the tin hat had become a dead weight, the heavy rifle seemed to be at least an eighteen-pounder, while the hefty boots were loaded with lead, and needed an effort to lift them for each step.

The mighty crag loomed bold and forbidding above their heads, and never appeared to come any nearer. Down below little bunches of houses hunched together in a blue haze. Rivers strung out across the dim country like grey ribbons disappearing in the distance. White campaniles, dotted at intervals, resembled dirty grey phials.

It was pure agony in the fourth hour. Every heavy, dragging step from hot, perspiring feet produced a groan of exertion. Runnels of perspiration ran all over the men's bodies—hearts were pumping like donkey engines, and the equipment cut into shoulders and dug holes in backs. Men had fallen out, and were lying on the track, with closed eyes and panting chests, and their friends had hardly enough strength to walk over them.

Meanwhile, the light had grown stronger, and suddenly the tops of the highest mountain in view were tipped with exquisite pink, which grew every second until the timid sun appeared, amid an irridescent veil of the daintiest colours.

" Sunrise-lovely-pink-tipped mountains," gasped Lambert, with almost his dying breath.

" Damn-the-sunrise ! " was the response.

The mighty crag came nearer slowly, and resolved itself into the actual mountain itself. Black dots became large huts. Lines of sticks were tall telegraph poles. When the journey seemed ended, a series of long, fairly level paths commenced which were more trying to the temper than the physique, but they eventually finished and the troops emerged on to a road winding round Carriola Valley.

They struggled, rather than marched. Every muscle ached, heads were dizzy with the strain, and the khaki clothes sticky and stiff with perspiration. There was inexpressible relief as the head of the column turned off the road into a rocky hollow, where the men were given refreshments and rest for a few hours.

A number of white and trembling men appeared an hour later. They had fallen out on the climb and finished the job when they recovered. Men strained their hearts badly on those climbs, and only those in perfect condition and of indomitable will could last out the journey.

Later in the day the men moved to a sector of the line that wandered in an apparently aimless fashion in front of shattered Cesuna, and was known as the

CLIMBING TO THE FRONT LINE 151

Cesuna Switch. It was an extraordinary district, which had been the scéne of desperate fighting, at intervals, for several years, and had for a considerable period been in the hands of the Italians. At one time the district had been a health resort, but its air was not quite so beneficial in May 1918.

Trenches started from a camouflaged road which transport was able to use in the darkness, and ran up hill and down dale along the wooded slopes of a deep ravine called the Ghelpac. These trenches were blasted out of solid rock in the most wonderful way, and the H.A.C. had to climb in full pack to their respective posts.

It was terribly hard work. Frequently there were seventy or eighty steps a foot or more high, up which the men hoisted themselves with groans and grunts of exertion.

The posts varied. Some were almost level with the edge of the trench and others were yards high, so that it was necessary for the sentries to climb ladders to reach the fire-step.

Lambert and five companions were located in one of these deep cuttings, and spent an uneventful night, taking their turn at the never-ending watch on the big cliff opposite, which the enemy used as a machine gun post at night.

Dawn enabled them to take their bearings. The mountain wall towered sheer behind them. In front, a steep slope disappeared into the Ghelpac, which was full of sparse bushes and large boulders, and from the farther side of which emerged a large bluff known as Stella Fort.

Sleeping accommodation consisted of a rough lean-to four feet wide and twelve feet long, containing the remains of four shelves. One of these was made of solid wood and was promptly bagged by two of the boys. Another had wire netting with a large hole in the middle and was partially broken away at the end.

The remaining beds were composed of a number of willow boughs, which wilted considerably under a man's weight.

In this shack, five men wearing clothes, boots, puttees and equipment tried to sleep after the night's work. Lambert and a friend laid on boughs together in a compressed mass of human flesh, inextricably mixed up with water bottles, bayonet scabbards and ammunition pouches.

After ten minutes' suffering, both decided to give up hopes of slumber and it took the struggling couple half an hour to extricate themselves from the puzzle, during which time the building swayed ominously. A part of the fire-step became the bedroom in future. As this was a foot wide, it became necessary to practise resting without movement, and when it rained, a waterproof over the head was an effective, if airless protection.

The H.A.C. sniffed about their new sector like terriers during that first week. Patrols wandered about at night seeking information. An unfortunate party of men, led by a young officer, was sent out at daylight to see if a machine gun post was tenanted, and were shot down like rabbits, a little incident that formed the subject of a lecture by the Colonel, which was listened to in stony silence. It was " Journey's End " in real life for several gallant boys.

An attempt was made to capture a machine gun team, who were observed to use a track leading to the cliff opposite. A strong band crept out one night, and after climbing a steep path hid themselves in a small bunch of firs. Firing was strictly forbidden ; the men were armed with wooden entrenching tool handles, and only a favourite sniping sergeant had a rifle.

The men lay on their stomachs and waited in breathless silence. An hour passed with no sound except the slight rustle of the fir branches. Heavy footsteps approached, and the sound grew louder as the

CLIMBING TO THE FRONT LINE 153

Austrian gunners drew nearer the trap. They walked right into it, and several British rose quietly to seize them, when there was a heavy explosion of a rifle.

The enemy turned tail immediately and bolted like hares. A few seconds, and heavy stick-bombs burst near the English party with thundering reports. Verey lights rushed into the sky, and streams of machine gun bullets screamed overhead.

The storm lasted for some time and then ceased, and the patrol stumbled back to the trenches without casualties but full of resentment with the cause of the failure.

Days wandered on, with their periods of heavy labour or troubled sleep. Nights crawled by with their interminable hours of watching, varied by occasional bursts of fury on one side or the other. The period in the front line was nearly a week, as compared with a day or two at Ypres, but except for the deadly monotony and lack of sleep, the sojourn was a picnic in comparison.

The Royal Warwicks relieved the men, and after a series of halts the H.A.C.'s stumbled down the mountain and arrived on the racecourse at Villaverla.

CHAPTER XI

THE ROYAL REVIEW

THIENÉ racecourse was very wide and straight for over a mile, and the H.A.C. pitched their "bivvies" near the top end. Lower down there were a number of hangars from which magnificent aeroplanes started at intervals on their various missions.

In a very short time the grass was dotted with small tents and there was a great issue of clothing. The weather was rainy and unsettled, but the hot Italian summer was due, and the British were to wear the eastern uniform of drill and sun hats, and included in the issue was a mysterious roll of material which was to be converted into a "pugaree."

"Bivvies" are narrow quarters for three men at the best of times, but lumbered with new clothes they positively bulged, and when all were at bursting point orders came to move to another field. The airmen had pointed out that the camp was likely to attract attention from enemy aircraft.

A great removal commenced. Up came "bivvies" by the roots, and with poles held high in the air, an imitation Indian procession commenced. Men were to be seen all over the district staggering beneath great heaps of clothes and equipment, from which articles dropped at intervals, or collapsed entirely periodically. The "immediate action" for the latter event was to sit on the wreck and curse heartily for several seconds.

The new spot was surrounded by trees, and had

evidently been cultivated during the previous season, as the ground was deeply furrowed. A flat bed was impossible without digging the whole interior of each " bivvy," and any men who contemplated this energetic deed were entirely prevented by the " pugaree order." The long rolls were to be unwound, folded and placed on the sun hats instantly. The " pugaree " was to consist of seven thicknesses, with a margin of an eighth of an inch between each. At back and front the ends were to taper neatly to one inch in height and at the sides the height from the brim was to be two and five-eighths inches. There would be a parade and inspection by the Major in the morning !

In times of stress, the troops consulted the drummers, many of whom were old " sweats," with much Army lore. Some had been to India, and these were promptly surrounded by a crowd, who listened to the directions with long faces and miserable hearts. . . . Shortly after the district was littered with small " pugaree " parties, each juggling with strips of flimsy material measuring many feet. The ends were held by two men who carefully folded the material into a third of its width, while the third pressed it with the edge of a button stick and wound it into a ball. The end was then carefully pinned on to the front of the " toupee " and the work of winding it on to the hat commenced. Another pin held it at the back, and so the troops went from pin to pin, and incidentally from bad language to worse.

Men with stubby fingers, or poor eyes for an eighth of an inch, cursed terribly or nearly wept. Throughout the hours of daylight, miserable soldiers sat singly or in lumps having a very hard lesson in millinery, until a flash of genius struck an excellent solicitor, but terrible milliner, and he proceeded to bargain with a drummer, who exhorted a terrible price, but obtained dozens of orders.

Unfortunately for Lambert, it was one of the few

jobs he did well in the Army, and he had a busy evening, but, unlike the drummers, made no charge. He returned to rest when darkness fell, but with head on one incline and feet on another, and body in a furrow, sleep was difficult. It commenced to rain hard about midnight, and each furrow became a miniature river. Nocturnal efforts to stem the tide were hopeless failures; coiling up like a snake or cat was not successful, and eventually the easy and only solution to the problem was to lie in the water.

A weary, bedraggled mob rose *before* reveille, and hung themselves out in the sunshine to dry. Wearing their usual khaki, but adorned with sun hats, they paraded before the Major, who tapped dozens with curt instructions to their owners to fall out, and rewind the "pugaree" according to previous orders. The drummers did a terrific trade, while the owners of the rejected hats sought solace in any wine obtainable.

Hot-foot on this trying ordeal came orders to clean every inch of leather, and to polish every buckle until it shone, and the blue sky of Italy became bluer. Some regiments may have enjoyed "poshing," but the H.A.C. hated it, and set to work with very bad grace.

Lives were not worth living during the next few days. Parades and polish were the orders of the day, and the unsettled weather extended the agony. A morning would open wet and cold, and the parade would be ordered in khaki. Shortly before the appointed time the sun would break through, and instructions would be issued for the men to dress in their new drill. Alternately the order would be for drill, and a shower would mean changing into khaki. As the same pantomime occurred with service hats and sun helmets, and there were long hours of drilling in review order, the feelings of the troops can be imagined.

Hundreds of them were literally dressed for the part they had to play. Equipment was taken to pieces,

THE ROYAL REVIEW

and were adjusted to a hole by officers, and woe betide the man who omitted a detail in the constant change of the costume. A lanky company commander added to his reputation by punishing a number of men for forgetting to transfer their shoulder numerals from one tunic to another during one of these lightning-change acts.

In the middle of this nervy period the sodden condition of the camping ground necessitated another move, and once more up came the "bivvy" poles, and another long procession of men started for a distant field, encumbered with mountains of kit and parcels of carefully polished leather and buckles which the men protected from mud with scrupulous care.

At last the terrible performance ended, and one sunny morning the 22nd Brigade stood like rocks while a tiny man, accompanied by a retinue of gorgeous officers, and a boy in a funny sailor suit, walked along their ranks and later took the ceremonial salute.

It was the King of Italy and the Crown Prince, and thoughts in a good many hearts went back to that other review by the Belgian king, which preceded their departure for Italy. Did this mean another journey?

CHAPTER XII

THE AUSTRIAN OFFENSIVE

MONTE GRUMO was a tiny hamlet standing on a hill overlooking the lovely gorge of the River Astico. It was reached by leafy lanes, and roads running through smiling country, and the sight of Camisino in the distance, nestling on the opposite cliff, revived pleasant memories, not the least of which was the fact that the desperate attack on the Val d'Assa, which had been practised there, had not materialised.

There were scarcely any houses, or life, in the spot chosen for the camp, and "bivvies" were the order of the day, but the monotony was varied by competitions of an interesting, though military nature, varied by boxing bouts.

Cut off from civilisation, the men had no news from the front, and everything was so quiet and peaceful as to be almost ominous. It was the sullen stillness that precedes the storm, and this one broke without warning. Early one morning the camp shook with the vibration of heavy shells, thunderous crashes came from the nearest village, which had been untouched for a year or two, vivid flashes lit the sky, followed by dull booms, sullen rumbles and murmurs resembling a heavy thunderstorm filled the air, telling their tales of violent drum-fire.

It continued for hours, and the men were aroused immediately. Orders were issued for equipment to be arranged in battle order, and the whole battalion to be ready to move at an hour's notice. Nobody

THE AUSTRIAN OFFENSIVE

was allowed outside the camp, and throughout the day, and the next night, the regiment was prepared for immediate movement, while the thunder in the distance rumbled unceasingly, growing louder and threatening at one minute and then dying down to little or nothing. That night a great glare lit the sky above the mountain and remained there for many hours. Evidently a " dump " was in flames, and men looked queerly at one another as they lay down on their damp beds. It was the look of men liable to be marched to battle at any minute.

Bad news came in the morning, and messengers rushed up on motor-cycles with alarming frequency. The Austrians, after a destructive barrage lasting many hours, had attacked in great force right along the mountain system and the banks of the Piave. Their artillery had pounded the whole front, destroying machine gun positions by the score, blowing up defences, stores and great dumps of shells and smaller ammunition. They had crossed the river, broken through the British sector on the Plateau and were marching towards the mountain roads leading to the plains.

Apparently the British troops holding our front lines had retired to rest when the incessant artillery attack had died away, and the enemy infantry had given them an hour or two in which to get into sound sleep, and then attacked suddenly.

Battalions rushed the front lines, beating down the slight opposition and blowing up our sleeping men in their dug-outs, while the main body had poured through gaps in the hills. The position was desperate. The Manchesters had been rushed up in motor lorries to help repel the raiders, and the H.A.C. might be required at any minute. That was a merry day. In addition to the uncertainty as to their fate, a sudden violent storm sprang up. Thunder roared and lightning flashed, apparently trying to imitate the artillery "strafe," while torrents of rain converted the camp into a pond with "bivvies" as lilies. In the midst of the cursing nobody realised the amazing part played by this tempest in repelling the enemy.

Messengers came hot-foot with news. There were whispers of reprehensible retreats by machine gunners and trench mortar batteries, but an officer had done great deeds in organising a counter-attack, and after desperate fighting the Austrians had been beaten back with heavy losses, and had returned from whence they came. Extraordinary news came from the Piave. The enemy had not only crossed the river, but were making substantial progress, when, without warning, a formidable torrent had swept down from the mountains, carrying away all the Austrian bridges and pontoons, and converting the river into a mile width of rushing water. The Italians had counter-attacked immediately, flocks of airmen had frustrated efforts to construct new bridges, and between the devil and the deep sea the enemy had had nothing to do but surrender.

Long after, it transpired that the unexpected body of water was due to a providential cloudburst or waterspout that had broken in the mountains during the storm so liberally condemned by the troops.

It was a glorious end to an unpleasant situation and the H.A.C. breathed freely again. Stories passed from mouth to mouth of an isolated English sentry who had sleepily presented arms to an Austrian battalion who had captured his regiment, or two company cooks who had " spotted " Jerry marching through the forest and put up a splendid fight behind an entrenchment of tins of dried vegetables. The news that the gallant officer and the redoubtable cooks had been recommended the V.C. and D.C.M. respectively met with widespread approval.

Lambert's joy at the news was soon tempered with disgust. Standing off the road with his back to it, discussing the news with some companions, he was surprised to see a horse pulled up, and to hear the group accused of deliberately ignoring an officer of another regiment. The reasonable protest that the gentleman had not been seen at all was ignored, and the senior was ordered to report himself to the Adjutant immediately. All the delinquents insisted upon accompanying this poor soul, and for half an hour the little crowd fumed and fretted outside the tent that served as Orderly Room.

Eventually the Adjutant returned with the news that the offence would be overlooked on this occasion, but that in future the excuse that an officer was not seen would not be accepted.

The party withdrew with their souls filled with a mixture of contempt and injured innocence, and their comrades expressed their sympathy in the usual way. When the incident was explained with fiery eloquence by Lambert, his friends laughed, and the hotter he became the more they guffawed. It always amused them to hear his views on Army discipline, and they were fond of recommending him to eat his pot of " Chickens' breasts in aspic jelly."

This referred to a bottle of these toothsome dainties that Lambert had carried in his pack for many months. On long route marches the edge of the bottle invariably dug into the small of his back and he had been tempted on many occasions to " dump " or eat it. On joyful occasions he invited his friends to join in a feast, and the invitation had become a mild joke in the platoon, but a long course of Army stew and bully beef seemed to demand nothing less than the end of the war before undertaking such an epicurean feast. On this occasion he refused to extend any invitations.

Ruffled dignity was forgotten when glorious news arrived from home. No details had been received of the fate that had befallen Lambert's brother in the March retreat. For three interminable months all had been silence, and persistent inquiries had elicited nothing more than the dreadful fact that he was " missing." The misery of uncertainty had radiated from the stricken parents in England, to brothers and relatives in Africa, Egypt and Italy, and had tinged all their communications with grief.

Now he was found. Just his name and address on the cheap printed postcard issued from a German prison camp, but it turned deep sorrow into ecstatic joy and Lambert's companions wondered, and inquired, if he had suddenly gone " potty."

The news converted a dark, threatening horizon into a vista of sunlit clouds floating in a blue sky, and not even the hurried packing up, and dreadful climb to the scene of the recent murderous incidents, damped his joy or quenched his high spirits.

CHAPTER XIII

A BUSY WEEK

TRAMPING over the recent battle-ground was a ghoulish performance. There was plenty of evidence of the furious shelling by the enemy, their short-lived occupation of our territory, and retreat before our desperate counter-attacks. In the woods leading to the front line, there were many new shell holes with the faint reek of explosive still clinging to them. Quantities of trees were down and many huts were in ruins. Elaborate machine gun posts were shattered to atoms, and the enemy artillery had evidently registered the lot, and put in some excellent shooting. One of the largest " dumps " on the sector was a charred crater in which not a vestige of solid matter remained.

The Austrians had raided a small canteen, and stripped it of its contents, but it had re-opened and was displaying a specimen of the ugly German gas mask, while a newly painted signboard had been erected over the door bearing the title " Jerry's Joy." In a bend of the road, near one of the gaps where the enemy had broken through, was a great heap of Austrian war material. There were rifles, bombs, gas masks, machine guns, ammunition, equipment, clothing of all kinds, and most of the latter did not bear inspection.

A silence brooded over the district. Both sides were sitting on their haunches licking their wounds, and one wondered at the thoughts of the deluded Austrians, as they examined the balance sheet of their final offensive.

Now that the horse had been almost stolen, the British locked the stable very securely behind many systems of barbed wire, and night after night wiring parties wandered out to the land between the lines, constructing every kind of wire entanglement, and occasionally the enemy could be heard doing the same thing.

A series of fierce raids commenced, and almost nightly the enemy lines were bombarded fiercely, and the darkness of the night dispelled by the most glorious Brocks' Benefit imaginable, until the devious trench system opposite blazed and sparkled in showers of golden stars and lovely colours.

Behind those showers of death crept parties of British, usually with blackened faces, and at given times they charged the enemy trenches with howls and yells, stabbing and shooting, bombing and blasting, and finally retiring with various numbers of cowed prisoners, whose faces gleamed white in the darkness. Every battalion in the line had to raid the enemy during the occupation, which meant three raids a week on a small sector, and a very lively time for all, especially the enemy.

It was a strenuous period, and to Lambert the adjective applied was far too mild. They were located in Cavrari tunnel, and of all the foul billets in a life of a dog that hole took first place. It was part of the mountain railway (supposed to belong to Cook's) that connected the large Italian cities with Asiago, and eventually Austria, and it had evidently been blown up, for there was a huge mound blocking the tunnel fifty yards from the entrance.

Rough boards had been placed on either side of the rails, and these were the slippery and wet beds. Over each was a tattered awning which previous unfortunates had erected in an endeavour to catch the unceasing drips from the roof. There was no light, even at midday, and the route for leaving or entering

A BUSY WEEK

the tunnel was by means of the single set of rails, with its multitude of nuts and bolts to trip the unwary. All cooking was done in the tunnel and the preparations for each meal resulted in clouds of suffocating smoke.

It was hard to analyse feelings. The incessant guards and "fatigues" were exhausting, but the misery of resting in the tunnel was indescribable. Lambert was only oblivious of his surroundings on one occasion. He was one of a small party detailed to carry rolls of barbed wire to the end of a system of trenches, and the memory of the journey is keen and bright years after.

The roll of wire was not a comfortable companion even on a mile of open road. It was heavy, suspended on the stick that was an indispensable accessory, and it had an awkward habit of attaching itself to the tunic or hitting its carrier in the ear with one of its barbs, but that part of the work was comparatively easy in comparison with the journey along the trenches.

They wound up hill and down dale for over a mile, a succession of slippery stone slopes and high steps. At one period the fatigue party would slither down a slope, with the burden on their backs bumping and pricking, at another they would be climbing up steps a foot high. Frequently they arrived at gaps blown in the trenches during the bombardment, and had to clamber over tall heaps of rock and mud. Men in tears reminded Lambert of the ammunition "fatigue" at Ypres many months before, and at their journey's end they were so exhausted that the kindly Company Commander allowed them to return by a short route overlooking the enemy line.

The party crawled back to the filthy tunnel beaten flat, and threw themselves on the wet and muddy boards without waiting for any food, and slept like logs for a couple of hours, until they were forcibly awakened and ordered to prepare for the front line.

Staggering and stumbling, the men climbed wearily

to their allotted posts. It was pitch dark, everything seemed to be wet, and there was a foul, unmistakable smell pervading the atmosphere. They " dumped " their packs anywhere, indifferent as to their ultimate fate or condition, and immediately mounted a guard on the fire-step.

A few minutes later, and five of them, including Lambert, were detailed for an outpost, and, climbing over the trench, wandered sleepily after a guide through a gap in the wire, to some heaps that appeared to be bricks or masonry. Here they stood, or knelt, at their posts for six hours. They scarcely moved or whispered, but stood like statues for what appeared to be an eternity of time. Minutes passed like hours. Eyes grew weary of staring in the darkness, muscles ached and ached until feeling disappeared, senses dulled until life seemed to have gone, and then they would jar violently into being, the rifle would be swung to the alert and a quiet challenge would bring the approaching company " runner," or inspecting officer to a halt. Like many sunny countries, the nights were very cold and frosty. As the morning approached, the hands and feet became numbed, and when the first rays of light revealed dimly the line of the enemy country, the outpost party could hardly walk.

A continuation of the road from the Cavrari tunnel crossed the end of the Ghelpac over a bridge and ran right across the landscape into the enemy lines. On the bridge stood a white house, which the outpost were to enter and use as a look-out from dawn to dusk.

Five weary men walked into the ground floor room and dropped heavily on to the smelly straw with which it was carpeted. They argued fiercely as to the first watch and completely disregarded the corporal's recommendations. Finally they tossed, and a man lay by the door, while the others slept soundly until aroused for their spell.

A BUSY WEEK

The enemy had occupied the room. There were signs that wounded men had crawled into it, and tin hats, gas masks, Austrian field postcards and similar military impedimenta littered the room. The use to which the shrapnel helmets were put need not be told here.

In the sunlight outside all was quiet. There was some kind of notice attached to a pole fluttering in the centre of the pockmarked fields, and the slight wind was rustling tall weeds that insisted on growing here and there, but otherwise all was deadly still and nothing quite so silent as the body of an Austrian lying across the road. It had been there a week.

During the day none of the men stood upright, but lay prone on the floor, dozing or watching rats playing an interminable game round the window frame. At night they returned to the trench, and took long turns on the fire-step, ending in the general " stand-to " at dawn.

There was hope of sleep in the daylight, but this ambition was not realised. Half the dug-outs had been blown up by the enemy, and were now the graves of their former occupants. Those still intact were half full of water, and Lambert was one of nine men housed in a large cave, which was half a pond, and in which two boards had been placed near the entrance, accommodating three men.

Lambert tried to sleep on the rocky path leading to the cave, but the combination of sharp rocks and equipment was too much, and he gave up the unequal contest in a couple of hours. Moreover, the character of the platoon officer was not conducive to slumber.

He was reputed to have been a schoolmaster in private life, and was a man without any sense of humour, but with an abnormal desire for detail. This was so highly developed that he was invariably asking questions, and usually asked them several times over. His men had had no peace from his incessant inspections and catechisms, from his first advent, when he examined minutely the whole of the hundred and twenty rounds of ammunition carried by each man to the day he left for England. In the line he had the men oiling bombs a few hours after " stand-to."

Sections were very short at this time, and nobody else seemed to be in the British Army. Many men were " down " with mountain fever or influenza, in spite of the compulsory sniffing of antiseptics, and the remainder had an incessant round of duties. In addition to many hours of guard during the day, Lambert was sent to a trench post alone, immediately night fell, and stared into the darkness from nine-thirty to twelve-thirty. An order then came for him to guard a gap in the wire in " No Man's Land," with instructions to watch carefully as enemy patrols were reported. That solitary job lasted until three a.m., and at three-thirty the whole company " stood-to " until five a.m. by which time there were ready to fall off the fire-step.

When detailed immediately for the " White House " outpost, it was straining human endurance to breaking point, but there was no opportunity for argument, and consolation had to be found in the best compliment Lambert ever received. A nervous boy, when detailed, had protested passionately, sobbing in terror before the uncomfortable sergeant, but had been soothed and reassured by the statement that " two jolly good men—including Lambert—were going out with him."

In all his experience Lambert never forgot that night. Sleep attacked him time after time, and for hours he fought it back with all his strength. He pinched his legs, knelt on sharp rocks, prised open his eyelids, watched himself like a cat, but after each effort his senses would become dull, and he would rouse with a painful start just at the second that sleep overcame him. The corporal spoke to him several

A BUSY WEEK

times on one occasion without getting a reply, but Lambert heard him from a long distance at last.

After hours of exhausting effort, desire to sleep died very suddenly. A noise like a door shutting, a point of light on the opposite hill, and a shell burst behind them with a thunderous roar and a shower of stones. Half a dozen followed it and the post rocked with the explosions. Lambert, crouching like an animal, looked up in time to see one burst in a flash of vivid flame a few yards above his head, and heard a large piece of the case crash into a hole in which a companion was watching. Agonised whispers came from the party, but there was no response, and it was not until the corporal crawled over and discovered the men alive, but winded, that the party breathed again.

The concussion stopped all their watches, and the fragment, large enough to cut a horse in two, had crashed into the side of the hole, missing the man's head by an inch.

Long guards and little sleep was, the order for the following day, but there was no relief for the exhausted body and mind. Hours dragged along, and to Lambert, standing alone on the fire-step, idly watching a prolonged, fierce fight between two giant ants, it seemed years since there had been any rest. When the message came that he was to form one of a defensive flank that night, to cover a big raid by another company, he laughed aloud, and stopped the fight between the ants. It seemed so silly for the insect world to be fighting as well.

At night a little party tramped over "No Man's Land," escorted by a cool, and popular young officer. They ensconced themselves in shell holes within a short distance of the enemy trenches, with instructions to fight any enemy troops that came out to intercept the raiders. "C" Company were attacking in strength at three a.m. after a heavy "box" barrage, which was to play on the front line, lift for the attack, and fall again after a specified time.

The flanking party were in position very early, and there was at least two hours to wait before the excitement started. Everything was very quiet, except for bull-frogs in the distance, imitating German sergeant-majors, and the incessant coughing of an Austrian in the trenches.

Lambert, lying on his stomach, wondered idly if the owner would oblige by coming into view and having his cough permanently cured, but it came no nearer and merely remained a blot on a beautiful night. Stars simply filled the heavens. The " Plough " was on its end, and Lambert reflected that in wonderful England it was on its side, and doubted mournfully if he would ever see it so again. A slight noise broke into his reverie and he found it emanated from his companion, a young boy who was enjoying a delightful sleep. Lambert, with memories of his agony at the " White House " outpost, let him sleep on, and kept a keen watch.

Out of the gentle darkness there suddenly came a furious humming, and a perfect storm of bullets whistled over the men's heads and brought hearts into mouths. For a few frantic seconds the uppermost thought was that they were spotted, but realisation came that the bullets were going the wrong way, and it flashed upon them that the sides of the " box " barrage consisted of machine gun fire.

The next instant there was a tornado of shells and they were in the midst of their own barrage. There were thunderous crashes all round them, and sheets of wonderful fire of all colours. Heaps of earth and stone flew into the air, and heavy clouds of suffocating fumes enveloped them. The boy woke up, and grasped Lambert's wrists, and they awaited the end together, until a tall figure loomed up against the edge and quite calmly led them farther back.

A BUSY WEEK

"Bit too near," shouted the young officer, with a grin.

The uproar died away somewhat, and from the distance came a slow boom of Mills bombs, the howls and shouts of men charging a trench, the firing of shots and screams of wounded men. "C" Company were into them, and it was a desperate raid while it lasted, marred by terrible accidents. One of our rifle grenadiers loaded his rifle with ball instead of blank, and the subsequent explosion robbed his friend of eyesight and an arm. A sergeant, climbing after two Austrians who had thrown up their hands, caught his equipment on a nail and was promptly shot by the treacherous enemy, who were in turn riddled with fifty bullets by an adjacent Lewis gunner.

About sixty prisoners were captured, and were being brought back, when, without warning, our "barrage" dropped again on the whole company. The prisoners broke and fled with the British after them like wolves, stabbing and slaying in "berserk" rage. One small sergeant killed seven men in a few minutes and received a D.C.M. to put alongside his M.M. Only one badly wounded prisoner was brought in, and there were loud curses at our artillery. Nearly every raid was spoilt by our own shells and nobody seemed to know where the fault lay.

Meanwhile, the enemy artillery had opened out and great shells roared over the heads of the flanking party, and burst with appalling thumps on our front line. One burst very near them as they lay waiting, but it merely dashed earth and stones in their faces, and after a quarter of an hour's "strafe" the music died down and the party calmly walked back to their trenches. The short retaliation was so unlike the German method that Lambert and the officer celebrated the fact on the trench top with a swig of rum. Later on, the poor fellow was to receive a wound that meant years of treatment in a hospital.

All things come to an end, and after another twenty-four hours' guard an unfortunate relief came into residence, and the H.A.C. tramped wearily along the roads to reserve billets. They subsided on to a floor that was actually flat, unwound puttees, and removed boots that seemed to have become hermetically sealed, peeled socks from pink and puffy feet, and slept, slept, and slept, until orders came to move again.

CHAPTER XIV

CONCERTS IN THE MOUNTAINS

DID you ever wonder why millions of ex-soldiers expressed their readiness to die before rejoining the Army? If so, it must have puzzled you to discover the reason for the seeming anachronism of men willing to depart this life at home, rather than enter a career where they might live for many years.

The puzzle is easily solved. During the late war the infantry were treated like children, or cattle. A few hours after the deadliest existence of mud and sudden death, they would be detailed to help any other unit in the Army, or marched out to practice platoon drill, and elementary lessons in musketry. The system froze the marrow in every man of intelligence.

One of the most iniquitous practices were the "cooker" guards. Immediately the exhausted men returned from the front line they had to take it in turns to rise from their stupor to protect the cooking apparatus throughout each night that the battalion was "at rest."

The H.A.C., when they arrived at Cavelletto, played at every game that they had performed in deadly earnest elsewhere, with the exception that the headquarters staff were decidedly in evidence at the rehearsals. In this gap in the mountains, up which the clouds rolled in an unending, monotonous stream, the poor fellows passed the weary hours in a succession of training "stunts" that were A.B.C. to experienced fighters, or took it in turns to unload thousands of shells for the artillery, from the *teleferica*, that brought them up from the valley thousands of feet below.

Huts were in deep hollows and one evening a tropical mountain storm broke. Rain descended in sheets and within a few moments a cataract roared down the slopes and filled the huts with water a foot deep. Cutting channels had little effect, and the best remedy was chopping large holes in the floorboards and waiting for the ponds to drain away. The huts had been built in the track of the flood torrents!

Resentment was deep and strong among the men, and it was with great joy that they heard that the Divisional Concert Party were being sent from the sunny plains below to entertain them. The "What Nots" were an excellent troop and everybody looked forward to their arrival.

Naturally there was no accommodation for a variety show, but the district abounded in enormous hollows, filled with sparse grass and huge rocks, and in one of these was constructed a platform, with a large piece of scenery nailed on the back for effect. It was the best arena in the district, but several shell-holes were filled with fir branches and there was a six-inch howitzer battery fifty yards off.

The arrival of a party in a motor lorry was hailed with cheers from a large crowd, squatting on all sides of a natural amphitheatre, but they died down when the sergeant in charge hurried up to an officer with a look of concern on his mobile face. Somebody had borrowed their piano and forgotten to return it.

Fortunately, there was an instrument of sorts in the Church Army tent several hundreds of yards away and a fatigue party was sent to fetch it. It sounds simple, but those yards were up a steep slope full of

CONCERTS IN THE MOUNTAINS 175

holes and rocks, and down another, and a piano was no light weight. The unfortunates expended most of their strength getting it up-hill, let their burden slide and bump down the incline, and eventually landed it near the platform wrong side up.

The "What Nots" made up in full view of the audience. Men in fearsome baggy trousers and khaki tunics were dabbing vivid paint on their faces between puffs at cigarettes, and the "girl" of the party, in pink silk stockings, satin petticoat, and army shirt, was alternately putting on garments and taking long draughts of beer from a mess tin.

A few flat notes tinkled out from the piano (which felt the effects of the journey) and the serio-comic came round the piece of scenery for the first time. He came round just a little too wide, stepped on a pile of brushwood and completely disappeared. Nobody had remembered to mention that the brushwood camouflaged a large shell hole.

Half a dozen men tugged him out and he obliged with "You can't do without it." As this referred to love, the audience could have told him that they had been doing without it for many a weary month, but it was scarcely the time for being critical. Evidently a large Italian boarhound disapproved of such a song being sung to soldiers, who were there to fight, not to love, for he solemnly stalked through the troops on to the stage, sniffed the singer from toe to knee, and then, throwing up his head with a disdainful action, marching slowly back again.

A popular turn followed—Lambert's friend, an H.A.C. corporal with a beautiful tenor voice—and there was dead silence as each note sounded clearly through the pure atmosphere. It was disturbed by a clattering sound that started faintly enough at first, but grew louder every second, until it became positively deafening, as four weighty gun tractors pounded along the road above.

They punctuated Kingsley's "Farewell" in the unkindest manner, producing an effect of this kind:

> "Be good, sweet-clank,
> And let who will be—clinkety-clank,
> Do noble-clank-clank-clank,
> Not dream of-clank-all-clank."

The men cheered the unfortunate singer sympathetically and the encore ended in safety. There were more cheers as the leader of the orchestra rose and faced the audience, a violin tucked well under his chin. He ranked in the Army as a private, but in happier days had been a prominent member of famous orchestras. This was going to be something first-class! Entrancing strains of a dreamy rhapsody came floating from the violin, when in the distance there was a faint whine, which grew louder until it swelled into a scream. The player's eyes left the strings and wandered uneasily in the direction of the enemy's line. As the shell roared nearer his head raised itself from the violin and slowly revolved until his chin was high in the air, and the item ended with a sharp screech that synchronised with a terrific explosion and a shower of earth and stones from the next hollow.

There were no casualties, and the audience had practically recovered when a popular Scotch comedian, flourishing an enormous stick, bounced on the stage with a whoop. Nobody felt like laughing just then, and his witticisms provoked little mirth, but they tickled an Italian mule, climbing a track to the road, who burst into a powerful and prolonged "hee-haw," that echoed round the great hollow. Everybody laughed then.

No doubt the battery-officer had hoped to leave the concert in peace and quietness for a time, but found it impossible to allow enemy shelling without ample retaliation. At any rate, in the middle of a saucy duet between the "girl" and serio-comic, there came half a dozen shattering roars that shook everybody in

CONCERTS IN THE MOUNTAINS

their seats, drowned the performers and nearly turned the stage upside down.

These disturbing events were calculated to upset the equanimity of most artistes, but British soldiers took things as they came (even if they were in the Divisional Concert Party) and the troupe commenced a rollicking sketch without turning a hair. It was proceeding merrily, when the one and only piece of scenery collapsed, and the entire crowd disappeared from view.

They were dug out and refreshments were administered but it was generally conceded that more entertainment could not be requested without appearing selfish. Willing hands were helping to pack, and the party were partly washed and dressed, when another heavy thunderstorm burst without warning. The rain descended with familiar violence, and there was a frenzied rush for the huts in which the Concert Party were by no means last.

In a few seconds the amphitheatre was empty of human beings but not of water. That rushed into the bottom of the hollow from a hundred channels, and in a short time the platform was an island in which bumped the piano, floating on its side, while the surface of the pond was dotted with a motley collection of wigs, clothes, boxes and mess tins.

A fatigue party waded in when the rain ceased, salved the " props," and when the sun shone next morning, hung the sodden garments out to dry on a long wire line. Quite a crowd gathered round two pairs of silk stockings, a satin petticoat, three dresses and a pair of corsets. They were strange sights in that Eve-less horrible place.

CHAPTER XV

A REAL REST

OVER everything and everybody in the Italian mountains hung a pall of grey mist and grey thoughts, which undoubtedly were a reflection of the awful happenings on the Western front. That glorious date in July, which saw the turn of the tide, and ended in the collapse of the Germans, had not arrived, and the H.A.C. wandered along to reserve trenches at Lemerle Switch like a lot of old men.

Lambert and his section were posted to a small log hut which had been erected in front of several shattered machine gun posts. The situation was decidedly Canadian. Fir trees abounded, except in the small clearing, cones carpeted the earth, and the smashed logs and débris gave an aspect of pioneer work in the backwoods. So much so that a spirit of colonisation filled the section, and as the floor of the hut was sufficiently bumpy to prevent long sleep, much time was occupied in developing the " estate."

Thin logs were discovered, and made into the framework of an awning. Wire netting was placed over the top and sides, and covered with fir branches to provide shade, and to camouflage the erection. Heavy logs were made into a rough seat and into the legs of a table, upon which a piece of corrugated iron was placed as the top. The tablecloth had been exposed to the elements, and was rather dingy, but the *tout ensemble* was quite chic.

A number of wild strawberries were found in the

A REAL REST

vicinity, and the section promptly invited their cronies to high tea. Lambert pinned a card, with "Strawberry Lodge" in large letters to the door-post, and the invitations were delivered in first-class style. It was a noble feast of tea, bread, and margarine of various ages, bloater paste, tinned peaches and wild strawberries with Nestlé's milk. Even the platoon officer smiled when he called to investigate the uproar.

In view of subsequent events Lambert considered that his luck completely changed at this time. He had never been able to sleep well in the Army, and for many months had awakened after an hour or two with severe aches in his hips and legs. In "Strawberry Lodge" this annoyance was very prominent, and one morning he was given permission to go to the aid post for some medicine. The doctor took his temperature, felt his pulse, repeated the operation, thought hard, and to Lambert's amazement ordered him to hospital.

It seems absurd to say that a spell in hospital was welcomed by the troops, but this chronicle is truthful, and, short of "Blighty" leave, which seemed as remote as the end of the war, it was an eventuality that was received with joy. Lambert was no exception to the rule. That night he laid in a truckle bed in the picturesque Field Ambulance, entirely alone except for the mice, that even ate the cover off a book behind his head, and reflected complacently that his chums were now wiring in front of the trenches.

Several quiet days followed at the F.A., farther back, and when Lambert anticipated a return to his regiment, the doctor quietly ordered him to the Rest Camp. It was an incredible piece of luck and the journey in the ambulance down the mountain was a real joy ride.

The Rest Camp was an Italian mansion standing in beautiful grounds, with a vista of magnificent scenery from the windows. A bed was allotted to him in an airy ward, and although it had partially collapsed, and the angle was somewhat sharp, it was a bed and he slept in sheets for the first time for over a year.

When the doctor ordered Guinness and eggs, upon the day that a re-directed parcel reached him (contrary to custom) the war was indeed a heaven-sent gift. The parcel contained an excellent box of cigars from India, which were distributed lavishly, with the result that the camp sergeant-major sent up to know who was smoking cabbage.

There were no complaints that week, or in the week that followed in the adjoining Concentration Camp. The weather was perfect, and just when money had completely disappeared Lambert met his old friend the tenor, on a deserted country road.

A loan was immediately granted, and partly dissipated in a bottle of *vino* while the old friends talked of old joys, present troubles and future hopes. Things were lively in the mountains. The Austrians were plastering the sector with twelve-inch shells and the H.A.C. were in the line.

Naturally there was a very mixed lot at the Concentration Camp, and the star artist was " Jock." His habits were horrible, but he had a flow of talk that was distinctly amusing, especially when the potent Italian wines had had their effect.

" I saw a picture of " Kee-chen-air," he told them, with a strong Scotch (or *vino*) accent. " It said ' Keechenair wants *you*.' So I came. Seeley fule. They told me I had to fecht for Bel-lgium. Och ! I'd like to cut the throat of the next Bel-l-gian I meet. . . . They say we're going to Pal-l-stine. I don't care. It only means lairning another language. I know sairveral already. *Encore botteel de vong blong? Encora bottilia dee vino rossa.* Och ! I'd soon learn the Jewish for it."

One night Jock took two hours to walk a hundred yards, came in with an awful black eye, and spent the night muttering, or shouting, blood-curdling threats

A REAL REST

directed against the whole Italian nation. The black eye had been received in a fight with an Italian soldier, but his account to the doctor of crashing into a window that had been left open was a masterpiece of detail.

The Divisional general, known to all as "Harry Tate," paid a visit of inspection one day. With hat askew, and hand to moustache, he surveyed the convalescents with a twinkling eye.

"Well, me boys. Well, me boys," he boomed. "Anxious to have another go at the Bosche?"

CHAPTER XVI

AMONG THE OUTPOSTS

LAMBERT reached the line after an absence of a fortnight, and found things very lively. The enemy were evidently fearing an attack, or wished to retaliate for the constant raids. They had brought up heavy artillery and the "strafes" at intervals were terrific and the atmosphere was distinctly "windy." In addition to the inevitable casualties, one poor boy had been killed in his sleep by a falling fir tree and the shortness of men was further accentuated by influenza, dysentery, and other complaints prevalent in the Army.

Naturally the same amount of arduous work had to be done by the smaller number of men, and for the first day or two the incessant watching and working pressed heavily on Lambert. It was soon difficult to realise that a few days before he had been basking in sunshine, with no fear of being called upon at any moment of the day or night.

The difference in quarters was particularly appalling. Instead of a bright airy ward there was a cavern many feet below the surface, reached by sloping stone steps, into which a ray of light never penetrated, and where the only sound was the dripping of water, and the swearing of men as they tripped over obstructions, or hit themselves against protruding ledges of rock.

The patient suffering of one man aroused Lambert's admiration. He was a drummer well into the forties, pushed into the company through the shortage of men, and his leave, after eighteen months, was due at any time. A large and particularly painful boil had reared itself on the top of a partially bald head, and the constant pressure of the shrapnel helmet caused great pain, but he positively refused to "go sick" as hospital would have delayed his leave. He stood the pain, added to the rigours of the front line for a week, until he collapsed and was taken away unconscious in an ambulance.

It is easy to be brave with companions all round, but a more difficult task when entirely alone. One morning, before dawn, the enemy suddenly commenced a terrific "strafe." Great shells screamed over and burst with appalling roars in all directions. To Lambert, alone on the fire-step, it seemed that his end was at hand, and despite every effort his teeth chattered, and his knees knocked together violently.

Footsteps along the trench steadied him, and he recognised them as belonging to the platoon officer. Judging his time carefully, he waited with outstretched bayonet, until the officer was almost upon him, and then challenged so violently that the man jumped, glared at Lambert and then commenced a typical cross-examination.

" What is the number of this post ? "

" Number four, sir."

" It isn't, it's number three."

" Corporal told me number three was washed out, sir."

" Number four was washed out. Now what's the number of this post."

" Number three, sir."

" Splendid."

Outpost duty was a severe ordeal at this time. The watch kept was of considerable keenness, but the number of enemy deserters who got through the system of wire and past the many posts was remarkable. Everybody was sick to death of the war, but none more so than the Czechs, and similar people, who had been compelled to fight for their enemies.

Our propaganda had marked effects on these soldiers, who deserted at the slightest opportunity. They came over fully prepared for a long stay. No heavy packs or firearms, but a light week-end kind of outfit, and as a rule they were found wandering about well behind the lines. One astonished everybody by giving himself up about three miles behind the outposts.

Another poked his head inside a cave, where a fat, good-natured cook was preparing tea for the troops. After a second's amazement, " cookie " jumped on the enemy and nearly crushed him to death by sheer weight.

There was no intention on the enemy's part of fighting, and he bore the burden calmly until the cook had searched him, and later consumed a good meal, and sundry swigs of powerful rum, with great gusto.

After cooking had ceased for the night, enemy and friend lay down together for a nap, and in the morning the cook cleaned up his rifle and bayonet, and escorted his smiling prisoner in triumph to Battalion H.Q.

Outpost work consisted of lying in various holes from dusk to dawn, watching the wire that divided the combatants. It was a cold, wearying job, and food was necessary during the long vigil. At first eighteen men were detailed as mess orderlies to this company, and spent the nights taking food at intervals to the scattered posts. Lambert, with a canister of hot stew strapped on his back, was guided by one of the outpost company along miles of rocky paths, through intricate gaps in the wire system, up hills and down dales. The guide had a disconcerting habit of not stopping when challenged by sentries, and after nearly being bayoneted on several occasions, Lambert discovered that he was deaf.

On the second night four men were detailed for the same work that eighteen had done previously, and

Lambert found himself promoted to guide. It was a doubtful honour, involving a walk of a couple of miles in the darkness, three times a night, through a maze of paths and woods that abounded in boulders and trip wires of all descriptions. It meant crossing a cemetery, full of shell holes, where little white crosses gleamed in the darkness, and finding tracks through wire systems that were baffling in their complexity.

Fortunately the weather kept fine, and Lambert found his two companions very interesting company. Henson was a gentle little man, with a soul full of music and poetry, who never hesitated to kneel on his poor bed and say his prayers in a crowded billet at such times when sleep was possible. He chatted about songs and books while carrying a heavy hissing canister of hot tea, up and down shell-marked tracks leading to advanced outposts. Robbie, a tall, hawk-faced man, also a music lover, but keener on " cushy " jobs and a little speculation, was amusing with his intense self-deprecation and insistence upon his demerits as a soldier.

With Robbie the " fatigue " was conducted almost at running pace, but with Henson it became an artistic ramble, and the discussions distracted Lambert's attention from his job on several occasions. He was guide, but invariably fell into the shell holes, tripped over wires, stubbed his feet violently on boulders or fell headlong into barbed wire.

On one of the trips he heard a loud voice talking in a dark coppice. Some hearty ring in the tones attracted his attention.

" I know your voice," he said into the darkness.

" So do I yours," came from the unseen figure, accompanied by a laugh that sent Lambert's mind flashing back eight months.

" I remember. C.C.S., at Istrana."

" Righto, H.A.C."

It was the jolly artillery sergeant, whose laugh

resounded through the wards, when Lambert had been "sent down" from Nervesa.

On another occasion the two men heard suspicious movements in the wood, and receiving no answer to their challenge, dropped on their knees and threatened to fire unless the password was given. There was no response, and the two men were about to fire when a voice inquired in unmistakable English: "Where's my ruddy mess tin?" The man had not heard a word of their challenge and was the second deaf man in one platoon.

Each morning at dawn the outposts came in, and the mess orderlies returned to the reserve huts. The enemy seemed to know this, and evidently enjoyed the idea of stopping heir progress by firing a few of their largest howitzers that were in a direct line with the road.

When their huge shells tore along this route the effect was paralysing to everybody using it. Shells overhead, rushing towards your front, or exploding by your ear as you lay flat, were unpleasant experiences, but twelve-inch "snorters" from behind were the limit.

On a long straight road in the grey dawn there would be a muffled "boom" from the tall mountain in the distance, a shrill screaming, and then the deafening, hideous roar of a hundred expresses travelling towards you at a million miles an hour, in a narrow valley between two high walls. A fraction of a second, and the monster was on you with an intolerable howl, and you were down on your nose, and it was gone, and you were not dead, but almost.

Lambert, who secretly prided himself upon his *sang froid*, fell as flat as a flounder upon his first acquaintance with this new enemy, and upon each subsequent occasion bolted like a frightened rabbit immediately he heard that distant "boom."

It was arranged for the mess orderlies to be free

to rest during the day following their night's work, but this concession was a distinct failure.

Structural alterations were proceeding with the huts, and no sooner had the tired men "got down to it," than the shouts of men, the banging of nails, and the dropping of logs and sheets of galvanised iron filled the air, and made sleep impossible. Protests were received with laughter, and Lambert was advised to seek consolation in his bottle of " chickens' breasts in aspic jelly."

That spell in the vicinity of the front line lasted for seventeen days, a long period for day and night watching and working, living in caves and pestilential holes, bearing the strain of frequent shell-fire, or " wind-ups " of enemy attacks. Rumour had it that the little colonel had volunteered to do an extra spell, and, rightly or wrongly, the men cursed at the mere mention of his name.

It was a terrible hardship for men to be filthy for so long a period, and there was great joy when baths were arranged. Fires were lit in the middle of the forest, where the smoke could not be observed by the enemy, and pails of hot water were emptied into the inevitable *vino* casks, which were so useful as baths in Italy.

Parties marched to the spot from the front line, undressed on the rocks, and walked gingerly over the prickly heather; but once inside the tub all the discomfort, and the fact that a shell might send the lot to blazes, was forgotten, and the parties scrubbed and splashed like merry children.

When the outside world seemed to have faded into oblivion news ran round the trenches like wildfire that the entire division was being relieved on Saturday, and during the whole of the day the enemy artillery were very active, and great shells plastered the roads leading to and from the lines. Time crept on and no definite orders came for moving, and no relieving troops appeared, but desperately anxious as everybody was to get away from the hateful scenes, there was a distinct feeling of relief in the delay. After a long spell in the trenches it was not nice to be killed on the way to a " rest " camp.

Orders to pack came very early next morning, and shortly after troops of burly " Yorks " arrived, with all the necessary impedimenta for a long occupation. There was a thick mist over the whole country, and platoons of infantry, units of machine gunners, trench mortars, and transport of every kind soon filled every road in the vicinity.

The district literally swarmed with goods and humanity on the move, and the enemy would have bagged many prizes if they had continued their " strafe " of the previous day. But not a gun fired, no screaming shells, or deafening roars disturbed the serenity of that Sunday morning, and the only untoward noises were the grinding of wheels and the panting of enervated men, climbing steep inclines with heavy loads.

Halfway up the mountain a dirty, grizzled A.S.C. man sat on a white stone, smoking contentedly. Two thousand feet below lay the battered wreck of his lorry.

"Boys," he said genially, " if you'll pull that bus back on to the road I'll give you a ride up the rest of the mountain."

Weary stumbles down the mountain, and long route marches in the blistering heat followed, but the platoon never went up to the Asiago Plateau again, and very few of them ever wanted to.

CHAPTER XVII

THE FOUR-PLATOON DINNER

The Vicenza hills were very lovely. Their fields of golden maize, profusion of dark green vines heavy with purple grapes, and bright colours of the picturesque cottages, all combined to make a charming picture for the jaded troops from the grey Asiago Plateau.

The sun literally blazed down from early morning until late evening, and even in their sun hats and light drill the British troops found movement difficult for many hours daily.

The "rest" commenced in real earnest. Day after day reveille was announced for the middle of the night, and the troops climbed about the hills, practising attacks and rearguard actions until their tunics were black with perspiration and they marched back to the billets like so many boiled owls.

There were no shells, but after some days men began to wish for the front line. Added to the violent exercise involved, there was the usual disappointment that the "rest" was a "wash-out," and hundreds of men complained bitterly that after their work in the front line they were entitled to more sleep and less work. The little colonel was blamed.

Very early one morning the Brigadier-General appeared on the rifle range. With the exception of the actual firing party the men were lying asleep in whole groups, and the General immediately inquired the time of the reveille. On being told three-fifty a.m. he expressed his annoyance, and sent orders that in future it was not to be before six a.m., which meant that the prolonged "stunts" on the hills received a decided check.

A delightful time commenced. The splendid regimental band arrived from France, and gave concerts almost daily in the verdant fields around Grumo, or in the twin village of Cereda, nestling on a ledge of the hills, several hundred feet up. Cricket, football and hockey matches were played in the cool of the evening, and the men derived much amusement from the Colonel's riding schools for young officers, who made noble efforts to keep their seats and dignity at the same time.

The only drawbacks were the flies and desire for leave. The former swarmed in millions and bit with a ferocity unknown to the home variety. They swarmed in black masses on any article of food left uncovered, and nobody could have had a siesta during the boiling afternoons unless completely covered with blankets or newspapers.

Desire for "Blighty," always very prevalent, became intensified during the "rests." None of the men had been home for a year, and many for nearly eighteen months, and the constant stoppages of leave drove the men to distraction. Those comforting letters from England, that were the bright spots in a miserable existence, openly expressed a longing for a reunion, however short, while the men who had left businesses found strong desires expressed for a brief return.

Lambert received an S.O.S. from the good friend carrying on his business, and with a faint hope stirring within him penned an appeal for special leave, which, to his intense surprise, was perused and passed on by the platoon officer with a recommendation. Similar requests by other men had been refused by Brigade, or shelved for months, and with the busy preparations for a social event the private almost forgot the matter.

Four platoon were a good lot of friends. They

THE FOUR-PLATOON DINNER

had shared joys and sorrows for many months, and the geniality and ability of the padrone and padrona of "Il Albergo dell' Olivo," which they had tested almost nightly, led to a suggestion for a platoon dinner.

The idea was received with considerable enthusiasm, and protracted bargaining in bad Italian led to an arrangement. For so many lire per head the good people would decimate, and cook a number of fowls, scour the district for eggs and potatoes, and concoct a chocolate omelette with rum sauce that would paralyse the most exacting epicure. White wine and red would be supplied in abundance, and the way the feast would be served was expressed with the most eloquent gestures.

A committee was appointed, and displayed terrific energy in organising a noble feast. Large purchases were made at adjacent and distant canteens, of tinned fish and fruit, sauces, chocolate, biscuits and similar luxuries. The canteen buyer found himself in honour to purchase Scotland's War Whisky, Italy's potent "*Caprari*" and Burton's Best Beer. Sufficient custard powder was supplied to the cook to make a huge dixie full of golden custard. Menu cards were designed by an artistic member, and drawn with much labour in a loft, with borrowed ink. Half a dozen of the band were roped in to play selections during and after the dinner. Flowers and ferns were "scrounged" for table decorations.

The carefully planned function needed many journeys up the steep slope leading to Cereda, and the dixie containing gallons of custard required a big fatigue party, but everybody worked splendidly, all promises were fulfilled, and a noble gathering of thirty odd sat down in a huge Italian kitchen to tables literally groaning with delicacies. The assortment of minerals, beers, wines and "*Caprari*" brought water to the mouth.

That dinner was a triumph of the culinary art!

While the sardines and potato salad were being demolished, and the golden salmon was being de-tinned by the Committee, the wonderful Italian padrone was roasting the fowls on a huge open fire in full view of the diners.

Lady helps had been raked in from the village, and were collecting and washing plates as fast as they were soiled. At the psychological moment the cook opened pots that had been suspended on all sorts of hooks, and with wonderful speed over thirty men were supplied with steaming portions of roast chicken, peas and potatoes.

Roars greeted the tasty food, and the uproar became deafening when the magician produced two wonderful omelettes, containing seventy eggs. Wine was flowing plentifully, and the chef responded to the many toasts with a graceful wave of the hand, and another little sip of " *Caprari*," which pleased him well.

A small room leading off the kitchen had been thrown open for the band, and sweet music came from the musicians, in the intervals of sipping whisky, which was their favourite beverage.

" *Pudini cioccolato con Rhum* " was the masterpiece of the dinner. A dainty dessert with a basis of eggs, flavoured with English cocoa and Army rum, it came as a revelation to palates murdered by stew and bully beef, and roars came from the company, to which the master responded with alternating bows and sips of "*Caprari*." Heaps of trifling luxuries followed in the shape of apricots and white wine, peaches and custard and red wine, nuts and "*Caprari*," cigars, cigarettes, more "*Caprari*" or anything that came to hand, while the band applied for another bottle of whisky.

There were no toasts on the programme, but a corporal rose full of words. He had rid himself of a few of these when the band broke into a lively foxtrot and the speaker subsided. Another young man rose with a roar that drowned the band, and proposed separate toasts of so many Allies that the company got tired of rising, and ignored him after the sixth occasion.

A glee party had kindly volunteered their services, and the door of the bandroom had to be closed while they obliged with tuneful quartettes. Wild howls for a speech from the chairman, from the friend of the Allies, was received with boisterous cheers, and the platoon officer rose. There was only a suspicion of a smile on his face, and when he started with "Comrades," Lambert tried to find something under the table, and remained there for the duration, with a handkerchief stuffed in his mouth.

At the conclusion of the peroration, most of the band were found to be still playing, but they lacked cohesion and seemed to be playing four different tunes. "Charlie," the veteran trombonist, with a red nose and watery eye, who smoked all the Army tobacco that he could "scrounge," stopped making noises when Lambert appeared and whispered in a very husky voice :

"Aren't we going to have anything to drink ? "

The uproar became appalling and attracted a large crowd of villagers, who flocked to the spot and discussed the situation with much vehemence. Several people attempted to make speeches, but "Charlie" usually took the opportunity of blowing a tremendous blast on his trombone. All the eatables had gone, and most of the drink, and as the steep hill had to be descended the company decided that the great and joyous evening had better finish.

As they started to rise, the Allies' supporter jumped on a form, and shouted in so powerful a voice that quite a number of people heard him.

"There's one ally we must not forget," he howled. "I propose toast 'Porshgall.'"

Something was thrown at him and he disappeared. The men streamed out singing, and Lambert watched the crowd carefully, to prevent the egress of the Committee, who were wanted for many jobs. . . . In a few minutes there were only half a dozen left, and Lambert noted an anxious look on the faces of the hotel staff. Their bill was for a considerable sum, and he mentioned the fact to the treasurer who opened one eye and then subsided into a chair. At this instant, the proposer of many toasts commenced charging round the room, roaring like a bull, and trying to smash things. Lambert chased him, gave him a clump on the side of the head, which sent him into a grinning heap in the corner of the room.

There was an appeal in the dark eyes of the padrona as she handed the account to Lambert. The terrible war had ruined their usual trade, and they had trusted the "*soldati Inglese*." He grasped the unspoken thought, and looked round for the treasurer, but that individual had gone.

A slight groaning from outside and Lambert found him sitting on the step, surrounded by most of the village. They were bathing his forehead and giving him milk, which did not seem a wise antidote to an admixture of English and Continental beverages.

With help he was hauled back into the room, and bumped violently on to a form. Requests, arguments or curses, met with no better result than the opening of an eye, and when Lambert went through his pockets and extracted a fat roll of notes there was no protest.

He was then put back on the damp doorstep to cool, and Lambert, after settlement, hauled the champion toaster from his corner and commenced the journey down the mountain road.

The young man bent in half as though punctured, and had to be held in the middle. Steering was a most difficult problem and before they had traversed two hundred yards Lambert's breath was coming in gasps, and he was bathed in perspiration.

A bright idea struck him. The man was a physical

THE FOUR-PLATOON DINNER

instructor, with a sharp word of command that was very annoying. Why not try him with his own medicine? Pausing for breath, he suddenly started with the command. " Left ! right ! Left ! right ! "

His companion pulled himself upright, plunged out a foot and marched quite well for a mile murmuring " Lef' ! Righ' ! " With help he was taken into the billet, and having taken his boots off and wrapped him in a blanket, Lambert performed a similar office for a bandsman who told him the history of his family for many years past, and continued long after his hearer had bolted. " Charlie " had not yet arrived home.

Inside the billet the platoon were engaged in putting themselves to bed. This consisted of lying down for a minute and then jumping up to see if some other chum was all right, and vice versa. Any men dressed were forcibly undressed and " dumped " on their blankets. Lambert was embraced violently by his neighbour, who insisted upon kissing him repeatedly and protesting his devoted love, and generally hubbub reigned until two a.m. when the kindly " Quarters " came up to remind them that reveille was at four a.m. for a hefty Brigade " stunt " in the hills.

" Charlie " had not found his way back by eight o'clock in the morning !

CHAPTER XVIII

"GRAVE DI PAPADOPOLI"

INTO the middle of that splendid time of feasting descended a bolt from the blue. The 7th Division were returning to France to relieve a division that had been shattered in the terrible fighting of the 1918 summer. Advanced parties had crossed, and all that remained were the arrangements for entraining a large body of men. The announcement was made by the Colonel, who added that they had had a good rest in Italy, and must now prepare for some real work.

Returning one day from an exhausting morning in the hills, with his uniform black with perspiration, Lambert was met with the news that the Orderly Room had sent for him several times. A chase up the hill elicited the information that his special leave had been granted, and he was to parade in khaki full marching order in an hour.

His head reeled at the thought of seeing that distant land of bliss, but within a couple of hours he had changed from drill into khaki, had dinner, packed with the help of good friends, paraded, received papers, tracked, and obtained money from the Lt.-Q.M., visited the Post Office, said *au revoir* to friends, and was away down the sunny road *en route* for "Blighty."

He heard of a train eight hours in advance of the one mentioned in his orders, and, after being violently sick on the platform, travelled for two days in the packed, but otherwise luxurious train through Turin, Modena and Lyons to Paris. Sixteen hours in the "Gay

City " gave him the impression that it had been taken over by Americans and Australians, and he was glad when the night's journey commenced to Boulogne.

The ugly rest camp was overflowing with leave men waiting for boats, but he barged his way into the centre of the first contingent to leave and crossed the Channel without troubling the various pass-checkers. London was a city of dread and darkness. The shadow of possible raids was heavy, and the Jews had left *en masse*, and yet everybody seemed feverishly anxious to have a fling before dying, and interest in the war appeared very jaded.

Hauling himself, and the weighty load on his back, on to a tram, Lambert bumped the conductress in the face with his pack. He apologised profusedly, and the woman snarled at him in reply, but he soon found that there were warm hearts to welcome him and, he basked in the sunshine of their open-heartedness for nearly three weeks. Home was heaven. His wife had carried on bravely and skilfully, and the family were in excellent condition, although slightly disappointed that their daddy was not in hospital blue.

The time approached for his return and there were the usual one-line communiques to guide him as to events in Italy. Naturally there was no mention of his division's return to France. It came as a shock to read, a day or two before his departure, that there had been great allied attacks in Italy, and that the H.A.C. had distinguished themselves in a fierce battle on the River Piave.

Once more lack of transport facilities had saved the division from the horrors of France. After weeks of waiting and " wind-up " they had marched to the Piave, and a post of honour in a daring attack given to the H.A.C. Behind the brief official news was hidden a story that deserves comparison with the capture of Quebec by General Wolfe.

The key of the Austrian positions was an island

called the Grave di Papadopoli, situated near the farther bank of the river, and separated from the allied shore by several beaches, divided by channels of water rushing towards Venice at twenty-five miles an hour.

A number of Venetian *gondolieri* under an Italian admiral were in attendance with large boats, and after several days' delay through bad weather, the H.A.C. embarked one dark night, and the boats swirled downstream. In those rushing waters the steering was uncanny, and very few boats missed the desired beaches.

There were three channels to cross in this mile-wide river before reaching the enemy beach, and one company had landed safely, if damp, when four red lights rushed into the sky. Almost instantly there was a scream of shells, and the crash of explosions, as they burst on the beaches. The work went on steadily in face of a tornado of metal that inflicted casualties among splendid men and officers, but nothing stopped the work, and eventually the regiment were on the island.

It was a perfect nest of machine gun posts, and through the entire length ran a fosse, or sunken road, which screened the movement of the enemy. Throughout the first night the enemy kept up a heavy fire on the beaches, while the British dug holes in the shingle, and sent out scouts and patrols to discover enemy positions. Hand to hand fights were frequent. Men were captured, and re-captured, several times in a night. Small parties charged into the very muzzles of the Alpine guns. Little men captured huge officers and big parties of the enemy. The Colonel was bravery and coolness itself, organising and leading attacks, and stirring into admiration feelings of quite a different nature.

One tall sergeant had an extraordinary experience. Captured on patrol, he was marched for many hours,

"GRAVE DI PAPADOPOLI" 199

and eventually imprisoned in Laibach, in Cariola. Shortly after the Jugo-Slavs revolted against the weakening Austrians, broke open the prison, made heroes of the captives, and invited the H.A.C. sergeant and an R.A.F. officer to organise a company of the rebels.

Beautiful as the country was, Italy was more attractive, and the two men managed to board a crowded train, disguised as two exceedingly sleepy Austrians. After many adventures they reached Trieste, to find that another revolution had broken out. After several hairbreadth escapes, they bribed the captain of a steamer to carry them across the Adriatic to Venice and eventually rejoined their respective units after a unique " Cook's Tour ! "

The detached, confused fighting went on for two days under severe conditions, but the Italians built a pontoon bridge, that was a miracle of engineering skill, and the transport, with much-needed food, etcetera, crossed immediately under heavy shell-fire, which killed and wounded men and animals.

The Brigadier was stunned, but definitely refused to go back; the Colonel's groom was last seen floating downstream inextricably mixed up with two dead horses; other good fellows were killed and wounded, but nothing deterred the British, who captured position after position.

"A" Company was in the thick of it. Good friends were killed, and the caprice of a large shell had robbed the world of a trio of delightful boys. They had been grouped round their Lewis gun in a hole when the shell burst in the middle of them. A little Welshman disappeared completely, and only his paybook was found. Another was shattered hopelessly, while the third, a keen card-player, was disembowelled surrounded by a string of bloodstained cards. The leader, a quizzical, satirical solicitor from Derby, had a rifle blown out of his hand, but was untouched. Henson disappeared from a patrol; and others distinguished themselves greatly in the protracted fighting. Nearly all the sergeants, and many lesser ranks, were ultimately awarded well-earned medals.

This company bore the brunt of a fierce counter-attack. At the end of two days the Austrians still held one end of the island, and had bridges communicating with the mainland.

In the rain and mist they assembled a strong body of troops unobserved, and suddenly launched a powerful attack. The company resisted them with the zest of schoolboys, pouring a stream of bullets into the advancing enemy. A Lewis gun jammed and the gunner attacked it with a hammer and whooped with joy as it came into action. Another " No. 1," having a similar experience, calmly " stripped," replaced the parts with exasperating care, and then lazily trained the gun on to the spitting jets of flame coming from an enemy machine gun, and silenced it with a short burst.

The Austrians faced the storm bravely for a short time, but it was too hot. Officers, cursing and beating their unwilling men, organised a few dashes without result, and suddenly the enemy broke and fled across their bridges with the British "potting" at their flying figures.

As the Italians had fled from Caporetto to the Piave, so the Austrians fled from it. They made one or two desperate stands but could not withstand the fierce resolution of the Allies, and the battle ended in headlong flight. The British chased them along the roads to the Tagliamento. Airmen bombed them unmercifully, whole Army Corps were captured, and for eight days the weary British tramped after the remainder, capturing large numbers of them, and great stores of material.

Every unit worked magnificently during this period, but it was generally conceded that the Honourable Artillery Company covered itself with especial glory'

"GRAVE DI PAPADOPOLI" 201

and the Italian Army honoured it by presenting each member of the battalion with a special medallion, designed by an Italian officer, showing the regiment's coat of arms and " Piave 1918 " on one side, and the figure of an emblematical boatman on the other side. This reached the men in June 1920, with a letter dated March 1919 !

It needed a book to describe the wonderful, yet bizarre, incidents of the period, and fortunately a fascinating and authoritative description has been published, written by the Divisional Padre.*

It is splendid reading but very misleading regarding the feelings of the British troops in Italy. It describes their chase to the Tagliamento as though it were a Bank Holiday picnic, but, in truth, the men were footsore and tired to death, badly fed, sleeping in the open without covering, and ready to drop with fatigue. More men died from the effects of exposure than from actual fighting.

On the long march they met " General Harry Tate."

" March like hell, me boys," he shouted, " and you will have won the war ! "

Eventually they reached the Tagliamento, waded several streams, and were approaching the opposite shore when an Austrian officer appeared on the bank.

" Go away," he shouted, " the war is over ! If you come any nearer I shall fire on you ! "

They had to send back to the Division to see if the unbelievable news was true, and meanwhile the H.A.C. spent the night on a sandbank in the middle of the river.

---

* " Defeat of Austria as seen by the 7th Division." Crosse. (Deane.)

CHAPTER XIX

CHASING THE CHASERS

MEANWHILE, the fortunate Private Lambert was one of the passengers in a series of cattle trucks ambling across Europe. The abominations, known as leave trains, were never noted for speed, and on this occasion the delays were appalling, and the journey to Italy took a week.

Oblivious of the fact that the delay was saving him from participating in the fierce, prolonged and final battle, Lambert soon chummed up with the other twenty-nine occupants, who consisted of representatives of dozens of units, and were of all grades of society.

The " Crown and Anchor " merchant who slid out every time the train stopped, and plied his business on the line, was quite harmless. The Welshman who had no cap, puttees, rifle or pack, accumulated them quietly on the journey, and the Gordon Highlander who forsook his kilt for the whole period looked odd, but lived on liquor without giving offence.

Two merry artillerymen were the life and soul of the truck. They brought back with them a doll with extremely pliable legs, and a stick in the middle of her back, together with a little dancing platform. To mouth organ accompaniment this puppet danced with loose-limbed abandon, amusing everybody on the thousand miles from Havre to Treviso.

The two artists were the finest " scroungers " Lambert had ever met. They seemed to have an uncanny instinct when the train would stop for some

CHASING THE CHASERS

time, and were away like lightning into the surrounding country, buying wine or obtaining meals. Time after time they seemed in danger of being left, but the driver knew them and they got back to the train, although on many occasions they had to run like hares to cut it off at an acute angle.

The train ran through France according to schedule, but simply walked across Italy in short stages, and delays became more frequent and longer each day.

Things were evidently happening up the line. A train full of padlocked trucks stopped alongside one morning, and fair, unshaven Austrian prisoners peered at them through the openings, and fervently blessed those men who pushed cigarettes through the bars of their cages. Similarly a Red Cross train halted near them, and the attendant volunteered a few details of the fighting. There were H.A.C.'s among the wounded, one of them an old friend of Lambert's with a bullet right through him, but he was sleeping and could not be disturbed.

Aftermaths of battle met them frequently as they crawled slowly onwards, and when the train drew up wearily in Treviso, there was a huge crowd of prisoners on one side of the square, guarded by the smallest and most disreputable Italians imaginable, and hundreds of repatriated Italians on the other, all yellow and sickly with privation, but singing national songs and hymns with the gusto of unquenchable spirits.

The busy R.T.O. hurried past Lambert and turned with a kindly smile.

"Your boys have done magnificently," he said.

The leave-party marched to a huge cavalry barracks, and, with the exception of bully and biscuits, were left to provide for themselves. In a very short time every scrap of wood available had been chopped, and the large courtyard was covered with fires and little groups of men cooking all kinds of foods and beverages.

Lambert wandered into the town and once again

ran right into the arms of his friend, the tenor singer. The "What Nots" had inherited some hefty work. The division was chasing the enemy, and entertainment had given way to employment Company work. Together, the two friends explored Treviso, and watched a large city arise from the dead.

Right in the centre of the war zone, its capture had been imminent. Within long distance shell-fire, and easy reach of enemy airmen, it had been bombed incessantly. Houses were down in rows, shop blinds and shutters hung in all shapes in the streets, and grass was growing between the cobbles.

As they watched, the town came to life. Every train brought back crowds of residents. Carts and traps poured in. Hotels, cafés and general shops re-opened, and although it was November, a smart ice-cream stall appeared in the station square. Within a day an apparent corpse opened its eyes and soon began to walk quite vigorously.

Money had almost run out, but the men found enough for an expensive, but most appetising meal. Shortly after they ran into Robbie, who had come by a previous train, and was penniless. It was impossible to lend him even a lira, but for old times' sake they stood him twopenny-worth of tea and biscuits at the Y.M.C.A.

One morning every flag in the town was flying and the sound of great cheering came from the Town Hall. Austria had capitulated ! Her armies had been broken up or captured, and an Armistice was declared from November 4, 1918.

The British cheered, and shook hands with one another, but it ended in that, as it was a very lean time, and practically everybody was without money.

The next day the leave party, composed of over a thousand men from every unit in three divisions, marched out of the town for an unknown destination. Nobody knew where any of the battalions were.

CHASING THE CHASERS

They had disappeared somewhere into the extensive track of country between the Piave and Tagliamento.

In a very short time, dozens of transport and artillerymen had fallen out, and the remainder began to howl for a rest. The subaltern in charge ignored the noise, and then lost his temper, and threatened to march the whole contingent with arms at the slope. The men jeered and laughed in his face.

Dusk was deepening into night when the party reached some Italian big gun positions. They halted in a village street, and a long interval elapsed before they were marched again, into a rutty field, and ordered to make themselves as comfortable as possible, without food and shelter, until the following morning.

Parties immediately scoured the district, and a number of the H.A.C. interviewed an Italian officer and were given permission to sleep in an old stable. The floor was very bumpy, but there was a roof to keep out the frost. Wandering about the vicinity, Lambert smiled at an Italian artillery sergeant who was passing.

"*Tedeschi finito,*" he said joyfully.

The man laughed happily, and, throwing an arm round Lambert's neck, led him to a heavily sandbagged dug-out which turned out to be the battery's canteen. On the way they took it in turns to announce the hopeful prophecy that the Germans were finished, and laughed happily on each occasion. That was the only conversation, but it was sufficient to add an excellent flavour to the glasses of liqueur that the genial Italian ordered.

Next morning there was a call for cyclists, and half a dozen men of the H.A.C. positively bounded forward in a body. Twenty men were chosen in all and were marched off to the Ordnance depôt and handed brown paper parcels. These were new bicycles in pieces, and an anxious time ensued for men who had not handled a machine for years.

Eventually the whole team were ready and set out

after the missing divisions. The cycles were terribly heavy in themselves, but with a pack and tin hat on the carrier and a rifle on the rack they became almost unworkable. It needed a trained dancer to throw a leg over the pack on to the saddle, and, when alighting, the front wheel reared in the air like a restive horse.

Brute strength was needed to push the pedals, and the condition of a man who had to blow up his tyre every ten minutes can be imagined, but it was infinitely preferable to marching, and the cyclists enjoyed themselves like schoolboys.

The route led across the wonderful pontoons dividing the beaches of the Piave, and along the roads which had been occupied by the enemy so recently. There was evidence everywhere of the deadly shelling of the British, and the awful havoc caused by our airmen. A bomb had evidently dropped into a crowded transport field, and the result was too gory for description. A mile farther on an Austrian lay quiet and yellow on the grassy side of the road, and somebody had taken his boots and socks. A horse's head and intestines were in close proximity. Evidently somebody had replenished larder and boot cupboard at the same time.

Tesse had been the scene of a desperate skirmish. The Austrians had made a determined stand, and had done a lot of damage before giving way. Plenty of evidence remained of hand-to-hand fighting. In one cottage three Austrians were found sitting in chairs round a table with cards in their hands, while the fourth lay across the doorway. All were bayoneted.

The church had been badly shattered, and in the churchyard, vaults had been smashed open and skeletons grinned up into the blue sky. A newly buried coffin had been dug up, but had been reverently reburied and the grave covered with lovely flowers. Captured war material and guns were packed in the square, most bearing the names of the regiments who

CHASING THE CHASERS

had captured them, and gun cotton and shells littered the fields.

The cyclists pushed on and kept meeting immense droves of prisoners, escorted by pitiably weak escorts. In some cases eight English soldiers were in charge of two thousand men, and one of the former, almost in tears, told Lambert of the rushes at mealtimes, and how he had had to shoot four men on the way down. One enormous batch of prisoners was herded by a General and nearly a hundred officers. They suddenly emerged round a narrow corner, necessitating hurried descent by the cyclists, half of whom fell off with a crash. The prisoners were desperate for a smoke and were selling anything for cigarettes.

Orsago saw the end of the adventurous journey, and here news reached the H.A.C. men that the battalion were making forced marches back from the Tagliamento. Lambert heard details of his friends' sufferings and endeavoured to buy wine, eggs or similar luxuries, but the village was stripped bare. There was not a particle of food or drink left in the district, and the enemy had even removed the church bells.

Thousands of prisoners kept tramping through, to camp in large fields outside the village. They gave endless trouble to their guards, and Lambert helped an old Italian woman to kick a raiding-party out of her cottage, who would have smashed down every door and torn up every floorboard for fuel.

Accidents were numerous, as bombs and shells were lying everywhere, and two of our soldiers gave up a comfortable couch in a stable to the victim of an explosion. The Austrian had touched a "stick" bomb, lying unnoticed in the grass, and the explosion had wounded him in a dozen places. The guards carried him to an English billet and left him for the night. The man did not murmur when his late enemies bound up the wounds and painted them with iodine, but lay throughout the night without a groan escaping from his clenched teeth. He was taken away in a cart in the morning, but not before his hosts had given him the best breakfast obtainable, and presented him with useful tokens of their admiration for his endurance.

The H.A.C. tramped into the village the next day resembling a band of exhausted brigands. Nearly every man wore an enemy bayonet or revolver, but with the exception of these trophies, the resemblance to conquerors ended. They had been fighting and marching for a fortnight, enduring every kind of privation common to advances or retreats, and were completely exhausted.

Only the fittest were there. In addition to the poor boys killed and wounded, dozens had " gone down " with influenza, pneumonia, etc., and news was already coming through of deaths in hospital. Nobody knew what had become of Henson.

Suddenly the entire war ended! As expected, Germany could not withstand the secession of Austria, combined with the terrific onslaught of the Allies, and an Armistice was declared for November 11, 1918.

The troops heard the news with comparative apathy. They were too tired to rejoice, and the country was like a desert, with nowhere to go, nothing to eat or drink except tea, bully stew and Army biscuits. When the official bulletin was published, with details of the frenzied rejoicings in England, they cursed the fate that had made them soldiers.

BOOK THREE
AUSTRIA

CHAPTER I

"BATTALION IN OCCUPATION"

UNREASONABLY, but nevertheless very forcibly, the British troops felt that they should return home when the war ended, and it was with feelings of profound disgust that the H.A.C. heard the news that they were to proceed to the Tyrol. "Battalion in Occupation" seemed to suggest a prolonged separation from home, and yet there was an element of novelty in living among the people who had been desperate enemies last week.

The trucks, full of men, jolted through the Trentino, along relaid tracks that had actually been in No Man's Land. Villages on either side had been shelled time after time for long years, and the stone houses had been riddled until they resembled crochet-work.

Lambert found himself in strange surroundings. To the amusement, mixed with disgust, of his friends, he had volunteered to take the place of a batman, who was spending a periodical spell in hospital, and for a week or two he had been cleaning boots, making beds, or packing and heaving a terribly heavy valise, and was now installed as assistant cook to the Major on the journey to Austria.

In the truck "Primus" stoves, pans, pots, dishes and cups were mixed up with blankets and kit. All day long elaborate meals were being prepared, or the dirty appliances from the last cleaned and scoured. It was no mean feat to cook four or five courses four times a day, and the head cook grew old in devising appetising variations, and filthy with catching pots trying to jolt themselves off the stoves.

The soup squares for the first dinner were very recalcitrant. Although crushed and mixed with boiling water, they refused to assume the desired thickness, and two hours boiling produced no change in their watery appearance. Patience was rewarded at last, and at the psychological moment, when the soup was hot and thick, the train pulled up with a hideous jolt, throwing the cook into the middle of his stewpot, burning his eyebrows, spraining his thumb and upsetting the whole lot. The jar sent the heavy iron doors crashing to, and Lambert thought his arm had completely disappeared.

There were three officers in the next carriage and Lambert acted as waiter during the varying mealtimes. While the cook crouched over the stoves, holding on to his stew-pans, his accomplice peered anxiously out of the door.

It required a steady nerve to jump into the darkness, avoid obstacles, and open a high door with one hand, with three plates in the other ; and the amateur cooks breathed a profound sigh of relief when the train drew up at Imst, Tyrol.

The hilly little town was in a huge bowl, entirely surrounded by towering mountains, and was composed of substantially built houses, very English in appearance, except for the wooden stairs and balcony which added a Swiss appearance. Everything was covered with snow, and the crystals sparkled like diamonds in the moonlight.

Orders had been issued for the British troops to carry rifles and bandoliers, and the officers revolvers, on all occasions, and any fraternising, or purchases, were strictly forbidden ; but these instructions were totally ignored from the commencement. As the H.A.C. marched into the village, to the strains of a lively tune ,the inhabitants came out to welcome them

"BATTALION IN OCCUPATION" 213

and literally took them to their hearts. Within an hour the troops were thronging the few shops and laying, in execrable German, the foundations of a firm friendship. The Italians carried rifles at all times, as between them and the Austrians existed a bitter hatred.

As it was mid-winter and five thousand feet up, the atmosphere was appallingly cold. With the midday sun at its height the temperature seldom rose above zero, and during the night it dropped many degrees. In most cases the billets were warmed by large stoves, or central furnaces, but six blankets did not keep their feet warm during the night, and the men arose with moustaches frozen stiff. Oxen emerged from their stalls with beards composed of saliva frozen into icicles, and despite spiked heels the troops slipped and scrambled up the icebound streets like so many ducks on ice.

The Tyrolese resembled the British in feature, especially in the shape of their heads, the colour of their hair, but the resemblance was more marked among the men than the women, who ran to fat very quickly, like their German cousins.

Most families had lost heavily in the war, and tales of incidents in the prolonged Izonzo fighting were terrible, but, being in a country district, the inhabitants had not been reduced to the starving condition of the large towns. The children seemed plump and well covered, but a crowd of them assembled at each mealtime with all kinds of tins into which they poured an indiscriminate mixture of any tea, porridge or bacon fat that the British did not require. After the first week their numbers increased to such an extent that the troops had to line them up in queues.

Palatable drinks were almost unobtainable. Wine was sour and prohibitive in price. "*Ersatz*" coffee looked attractive, but left a strong thirst, and the British speedily turned their attention to fruit drinks or tea "*mit Rhum.*" In one of the *gasthofs* the waitress produced a bottle and asked Lambert if it was " gute " ! She was astounded when he whooped for joy, and promptly mixed a measure with water. It was a pre-war bottle of Robertson's Highland Whisky, and the mere mention of the incident sufficed to bring a crowd of anxious inquirers. For days Lambert was stopped by men of all companies and asked where *the* whisky could be obtained.

Immediately the British marched in, sentry posts were installed in state. With all the ceremonial of pre-war times guards were changed daily, and woe betide the individual who was not " poshed " to the eyebrows. The foxy-faced adjutant prided himself upon his preliminary inspection, and even looked behind buttons to see if any cleaning material remained.

Every day at noon the new and old guards stood in the snow while the farce proceeded. It lasted for nearly half an hour, while the guards stood with frozen feet and burning hearts until the time came to slip and slide (with fixed bayonets) to the square for dismissal, or to adjourn to the guardroom for their twenty-four hours' ordeal. Several seasoned soldiers fainted through the great cold, which made constant motion imperative, and during the glistening, frozen night two hours tramping to and fro did not warm the members.

Instinct seemed to have guided Lambert in applying for his menial job. While the cleaning of wet boots, " scrounging " of coal and wood for fires, preparation of hot water for baths, and periodical " washing up " for hours on end involved a considerable amount of unusual work, it preserved him, for a time, from the " guards " torture and made an indulgence in the local sports possible.

Everybody in the district tobogganed. Tiny babies or decrepit grandmothers slid down the steep streets with equal dexterity. Women delivering washing, or doing their shopping used toboggans, and it took

"BATTALION IN OCCUPATION" 215

" Tommy " about five minutes to decide that this was the sport for him. Babies, or elderly folk, were bribed with chocolate for the loan of their vehicles, and henceforth every hill in the town, and out of it, resounded with warning howls from flying parties.

At first hundreds of men whizzed down the narrow main streets, until a party dashed into the Italian General and his staff, who were leaving their headquarters, and the resulting loss of balance, and dignity, led to an immediate " *Verboten*."

The best sport was then found on a steep slope, promptly named the Cresta Run, which had sharp turns at the beginning and end, with a ten foot drop for the unskilful at the top and a dangerous fence running at right angles at the bottom. It was not until the spills were numbered in hundreds, and casualties became frequent, that the popular venue became the Landeck Road, which provided a great run of a mile, with four exciting, but easier turns.

Landeck was sixteen kilos away, and Lambert and Robbie, also a batman, promptly journeyed there on a tour of inspection. After commiserating with the station guard, huddled round a fire in the waiting-room, they boarded a train, and, calmly ignoring all railway officials, travelled a dozen miles in the usual overheated Austrian train.

The town was larger than Imst, but not so beautiful, and its winding streets were packed with Italian soldiers. They all stared hard at the Britishers, and the native population gazed at them in amazement. It was evident that the English enemy were not familiar sights, and little children followed in their footsteps as they wandered about sampling the execrable food and drink that the place had for sale. Some of the former nearly killed Robbie, and a particular brand of " schnapps," that resembled paraffin, disorganised Lambert, who decided upon a nap on a wooded bench in one of the many *gasthofs*.

Later he insisted that a word of about seventy letters meant "Museum," and dragged his unwilling companion up steep flights of steps to the door of a pretentious house, which proved to be the residence of the Mayor.

On the way back to the station the men overtook an attractive Austrian lady, with a pretty little girl, struggling along with heavy bags. They saluted with a gallant sweep, and insisted upon relieving her of the articles, which they duly deposited on the platform. To their amazement, the lady promptly offered them a kronen note each, which they declined, to her evident embarrassment.

When Christmas was imminent, Imst had become quite a centre for Austrian tourists, who came from long distances to view the English ; watch the changing of the guard which local papers compared with similar functions in Potsdam, and invariably helped to swell the crowded audiences at the concerts given by the band, whose fame spread throughout the district. It was illuminating to see crowds of Austrians standing while the band played British, French and Italian National Anthems.

By this time the Tyrolese and British were fast friends, but the culminating point came when leaflets, printed in excellent English, were distributed to the troops, asking them to use their influence with the British Government in an endeavour to make the Austrian Tyrol a British Dominion.

Christmas Day saw a mighty spread similar to the one provided in Italy a year ago. Out of the canteen profits tremendous purchases of turkeys, etc., had been made in Italy, and the long tables groaned with a good old English dinner. When everybody was replete with food and beer, there were cheers for the little Colonel, who made a farewell speech, and a thunderous roar for "Major Nobby," who was a great favourite in spite of his apparent ferocity.

"BATTALION IN OCCUPATION" 217

It was all over in the early afternoon, and most of the men settled down to slumber. Lambert mooned about headquarters with the desire for home and family gnawing at him like a hungry fox. His feet itched, and his hands clenched at the sounds of waltzes and fox-trots, until in desperation he clapped on his hat and charged out into the freezing night.

In the darkness he bumped into a man zig-zagging about with a toboggan, who immediately invited him to come for a run on the "Cresta." This was now considered dangerous in the daylight, and at night a crash seemed inevitable, especially with an inebriated companion. But the misery of Christmas in the Army demanded action of some sort, and the danger rendered the adventure quite an attractive one.

The reveller insisted on steering, and the two men rounded the corner on one runner amidst a shower of snow. Down the straight they went, with the icy wind stinging their faces, and whistling past their ears, and Lambert waited for the crash when they charged the stout fencing at the bottom. Suddenly there was a jolt, and he was pitched violently over his companion's head, but instead of a sickening collision with solid wood, he landed upon a bed of delightful softness that enveloped him in a cold embrace.

The steersman had fortunately run clean off the track, and the whole affair had dropped into a snow drift seven or eight feet deep. It cooled their ardour, and scrambling out they returned to their scarcely warmer beds at Headquarters.

CHAPTER II

DEMOBILISATION

DEMOBILISATION commenced in earnest after Christmas. Students and school teachers were the first to go, and these naturally comprised many young men without wives, families, or other responsibilities. The order happened to include most of the new draft from England, who reached the regiment after the fighting was over, and disgust was forcibly expressed at such an absurdity. One of the young fellows expostulated.

" Look at the rotten journey we had ! " he announced.

Lambert returned to his company when his officer's batman was discharged from hospital, and plunged headlong into a mixture of " guards," tobogganing, and ski-ing that composed their life. He found the companies seething with discontent, seeking to forget the exhausting routine of sentry-go, and the desire for England, by every possible evasion of discipline and furious indulgence in the winter sports.

The Italians had kindly supplied fifty toboggans and pairs of skis, which were lent to the companies " off duty," and the whole district resounded day and night with the scream of iron runners on ice, and the laughter of men ski-ing. On the steep slopes men were to be seen in every imaginable position ; rushing down the mountain sides with eyes strained out of their sockets in the effort to keep the balance ; lying on backs with legs waving in the air ; or on their sides, making desperate efforts to get a foothold on the slippery surface.

DEMOBILISATION 219

Getting up after a tumble was a desperate matter. When the seven foot slats of pine had been disengaged from the back of the ears, it took anything from a minute to a day to get on the feet again, and epochs to reach the hilltop.

The snow was wonderfully soft, and although frozen lumps were forced by the terrific falls inside the tops of tunics, the sport warmed the men up like no other exercise, and a few hours' ski-ing was funnier than any pantomime in the history of mime.

Men on duty saw the black spots on the mountain sides, and cursed as they tramped their beats. They had to march about like machines for many weary hours, and spend the intervals in the guardroom, wearing full equipment, on the *qui vive* for a sudden turn-out. The rigour of these guards depended largely upon the temperament of the sergeant. If "windy" the ordeal was hateful, but a calm chief made the job more bearable, and allowed "miking" at quiet moments.

A corporal of the former variety was chipped for weeks for calling the step at three a.m. to the new guards slipping and sliding on the icy streets. One of the other kind laughed heartily when it was necessary to drag Robbie away from a band concert, when he should have been parading the front of the building.

During the Christmas period the Austrians were going very strong with carol singers and parties of men wearing half a dozen large bronze bells, who jumped through the town like maniacs at all hours of the night, scaring away evil spirits, and incidentally disturbing everybody's slumber.

One night they awoke the Major, who descended from his room to ascertain the cause of the uproar, and took the opportunity of seeing how the guard was being maintained.

The sentry outside the entrance had disappeared to watch the movements of a lady, who evidently could not sleep. Inside the guardroom the men were dozing beneath their blankets, and the men were aware of the Major's basilisk eye fixed on the heap of equipment and boots that had been removed in defiance of orders.

A terrific row ensued, during which the Major sent a messenger summoning the R.S.M., and another cancelling the order. All the guards were threatened with instant arrest, and the sergeant was accused of not visiting the various sentry posts for hours.

This individual, a tall calm youth of twenty, did not bend before the storm. He swore emphatically that he had visited all posts within the last hour, contradicted the Major to his face when the officer swore otherwise, and bravely defended the incriminating glass of " grog," by saying that the lack of hot refreshment in the middle of an Arctic night was a disgrace to the Army. The Major retired at this thrust, vowing court-martial for all in the morning.

He stalked into the guardroom after breakfast, accompanied by the Adjutant, while the chastened sentries watched furtively. The two officers stalked about the room measuring and pointing, and left without any of the lurid threats being enforced. Later pioneers arrived, and fixed a large copper, and cooks dispensed hot cocoa nightly to all subsequent guards !

The H.A.C. were quite detached from the Army during their occupation at Imst. All food was packed into trucks in Italy, and guarded on the journey to Austria by their own men, and there were short rations when the Brenner Pass had its regular landslip. They organised their own postal service, and letters were taken to, and fetched from Verona daily by two men each way. The " post fatigue " was eagerly sought after, and Lambert was delighted when he was detailed. It meant five days rest from the guards, and the brief sojourn in sunny Italy was a delightful contrast, after the dead white iciness of the Tyrolese Alps.

DEMOBILISATION

On Innsbruck Station a man in Austrian uniform walked up to him.

"Do you know Henson," he asked in stilted English. Lambert jumped.

"Good Lord, yes!" he said excitedly. "Is he alive?"

Henson was alive, and well. When his section had retired during the island battle, he had fallen into a shell hole, and shortly after one of the advancing Austrians had fallen on top of him. Instead of keeping still, he had struggled to get out first, and had been captured. Weak and very ill, he had been unable to march, and the Austrians had promptly sent him to hospital at Kleinfurt, where Lambert's interrogator had been in the next bed, and, speaking good English, had interpreted and generally acted as a good Samaritan.

Lambert was overjoyed at the news, and cordially invited the Austrian over to Imst upon his return, and later he entertained the man and his plump fiancée, as lavishly as possible, to the horror of his officers and amusement of the men. Meanwhile, he consented to help him by smuggling cotton from Italy. Reels cost approximately 1s. 8d. each in Verona, and fetched between 10s. and 15s. in Innsbruck, and out of the profits the Austrian was saving for a civilian suit, which cost about £25.

The journey to Verona took two days, during which time the train crawled up the Brenner Pass, and down through the Trentino, where the Italians had already replaced the Austrian names of the stations with the old Italian names. Crowds of Italian officers were travelling to Italy, and it was a popular amusement for the British "Tommies" to keep them out in the corridor by stolid insistence upon the meaning of "*Riservata per Postale Inglese*," which with the compartment was labelled. It was an idea conceived by the first "fatigue," and although there had been no official sanction, the move was a bright and most effective one.

A day in Verona among the restaurants and sunny streets, an evening at the Opera, the purchase of little luxuries for friends, and cotton for the enemy, and the journey back commenced.

The British element at Imst seethed during the next few weeks. Demobilisation was proceeding slowly, but steadily, and hopes of home were coming nearer, when the new Army Act was passed and there was an uproar. No men were to be demobilised who had come on active service after January 1916.

It affected nearly every man in the regiment. Scarcely half a dozen had survived the battles during that period. The Division had had some 67,000 casualties, which meant that over two divisions had disappeared; hardly a man of the 1915 contingent remained, and even the lucky survivors of the Bullecourt and Passchendaele slaughters were outside the period named in the order, which to any person with a grain of knowledge revealed itself as benefiting only those units who had been behind the lines, while the "foot-sloggers" were being periodically carved into ribbons.

Deep gloom, or furious rage, seized everybody. Men who had tramped across countries, lived in mud and blood, endured the hell of trenches, and plunged through tornadoes of shot and shell without undue fuss, howled curses upon the War Office, and wished frightful deaths to Winston Churchill. Men with wives, families and businesses waiting for them bearded their Company officers with ill-concealed insolence, bombarded the various Adjutants, and took every opportunity of expressing their opinions to the Colonel and Major.

Blank despair settled upon Lambert. His partner in London had applied for his discharge, which had been granted, and he had been anticipating release at any

DEMOBILISATION

moment. Now all hope disappeared, and it seemed that freedom would never come.

Feverishly he examined the verbose, intricate wording of the Act, found a clause referring to one-man businesses, fanned himself into an ecstacy of fury, and, with a boon companion, hurtled over to Headquarters to argue the matter with the Adjutant. Army Act in hand he bearded the officer and started his speech, but the Adjutant stopped him dead.

" You're Lambert, aren't you ? " he said curtly. " Z16 has come through, and you go to-morrow ! "

His farewell to the regiment was an inglorious one. The draft were paraded before the Regimental-Sergeant-Major, known affectionately as " Erb," or " The Duke of Guernsey." He wished to shake hands with the parting men, but Lambert misunderstood the gesture, and nearly hit him on the nose with his rifle.

The bright blue eyes recognised him as the man who had been " run " months before, for parading in front of headquarters, at 5 a.m., with his rifle slung over his shoulder.

" 'E ain't very bright, is 'e ? " he queried of the onlookers.

" Wind-up " had not been a characteristic of Lambert's army career, but the journey to England, with its many interruptions, was a perfect nightmare of fear. The week's delay at Monttecchio Maggiore (over which towered the ruins of Romeo's and Juliet's castle) when every hour brought its rumour of cancelled train or a new Army Order, was a misery which was only forgotten during an idyllic day among the wonders of Venice.

The fear that the forbidden Austrian revolver hidden down his trousers would be discovered, and the punishment of cancelled demobilisation enforced. The monotony, now magnified a thousand times, of the week's journey in trucks, and the terrible days at Harfleur Camp, where delousing and waiting were the sole occupations, produced a state of mind that had not been apparent during the hottest shelling, or the most prolonged period of trench life.

At long last the contingent boarded a smart American steamer, and Lambert spent his last five francs as a tip for a sleep in the officers' mess. In the early morning they entered Southampton Docks, and an hour or two later the troop train crawled out of the station.

A burly cockney was leaning out of the window as they puffed slowly alongside the streets of Southampton. Suddenly he howled in excitement, and pointed to a man pushing a barrow filled with vegetables.

" Oh! my great gawdfathers," he howled. " It's bloomin' old England agin. Look at that barrer! Hi! F-I-N-E H-E-A-R-T-Y B-R-O-C-K-E-R-L-O-W."

THE END

JOHN LONG LTD., PUBLISHERS, LONDON, ENGLAND. 1930.
PRINTED BY THE ANCHOR PRESS LTD., TIPTREE, ESSEX, ENGLAND.

www.ingramcontent.com/pod-product-compliance
Lightning Source LLC
Chambersburg PA
CBHW021327190426
43193CB00039B/217